THERE STOOD A BLUE BOWL FILLED WITH FERNS
AND VIOLETS

A YANKEE GIRL
AT
GETTYSBURG

By

ALICE TURNER CURTIS

AUTHOR OF

"*The Little Maid*" *Historical Books*
&
"*Yankee Girl*" *Civil War Stories*

Illustrated by
CHARLES GARNER

APPLEWOOD BOOKS
BEDFORD, MASSACHUSETTS

A Yankee Girl at Gettysburg was first published by the Penn Publishing Company in 1926. Applewood Books would like to thank Phyllis Butters for lending her copy of *A Yankee Girl at Gettysburg* for reproduction.

ISBN 1-55709-526-4

Thank you for purchasing an Applewood Book.
Applewood reprints America's lively classics—
books from the past that are still of interest to modern readers.
For a free copy of our current catalog, write to:
Applewood Books, P.O. Box 365, Bedford, MA 01730.

10 9 8 7 6 5 4 3 2 1

Printed and bound in Canada.

Library of Congress Cataloging-in-Publication Data
Curtis, Alice Turner.
    A Yankee girl at Gettysburg / by Alice Turner Curtis;
illustrated by Charles Garner.
        p.   cm.
    Summary: In the early summer of 1863, eleven-year-old
Kathleen Webb finds herself involved in several memorable
adventures in the days leading up to the decisive Civil War
battle at Gettysburg.
    ISBN 1-55709-526-4
    1. Gettysburg (Pa.), Battle of, 1863—Juvenile fiction.
[1. Gettysburg (Pa.), Battle of, 1863—Fiction. 2. United
States—History—Civil War, 1861–1865—Campaigns—Fiction.]
I. Garner, Charles, ill.   II. Title.
PZ7.C941Yang   1999b
[Fic]—dc21

                            98-56022
                              CIP
                              AC

CONTENTS

ILLUSTRATIONS

A Yankee Girl at Gettysburg

CHAPTER I

A BIRTHDAY VISIT

"ELEVEN years old! Eleven years old!"

Kathleen Webb repeated these three words over and over to herself as she rode happily along the highway that led from her home to the pleasant town of Gettysburg. She endeavored to sit up as straight and tall as possible on the seat beside her father, and now and then would look a little questioningly at his grave face and wonder if it could be possible that her father had forgotten that this was the fifteenth day of April, and that his only daughter was now eleven years of age.

But of course he could not have forgotten it, because was he not taking her to Gettysburg as a special birthday treat to spend the day with Aunt Melvina Stevens? And remembering this delightful fact Kathleen bounced up and down on the broad seat and suddenly clasping both hands about her father's arm exclaimed:

"And Aunt Melvina always has birthday 'surprises'! Last year it was this locket," and her clasp on her father's arm relaxed as her hand reached up to touch the small gold locket that swung on its slender chain around her neck. "And what do you suppose 'twill be to-day, Father?" and Kathleen's blue eyes looked up at her father with such apparent delight in the fact that it was her own special day when unexpectedly pleasant things were bound to happen, that Mr. Webb smiled down at her and for the moment forgot his own anxious thoughts and said:

"Who knows what Aunt Melvina has planned! But do not forget that you have a gift for her; and I'll wager she will be well pleased with it. You can tell your aunt that she can thank your Yankee grandmother for teaching you how to make a hooked rug."

"Is Grandma Webb a 'Yankee'?" asked Kathleen, her thoughts flying back to the village on the Maine coast that had been her home until she was eight years old, and where her Grandmother and Grandfather Webb still lived.

"Of course she is, and so are you, and so am I," declared her father. "If being a 'Yankee' means loyalty to the United States," he added as if to himself.

"Do you like Gettysburg as well as Bloomville, Father? Ted says he'll wager there's not another town in Pennsylvania that is the centre of a wheel!" and

Kathleen gave a little chuckle as she remembered her brother's drawing a picture of the town as if it was in reality the hub of a wheel, with its eleven different roads radiating from it like spokes of a wheel.

"Ted is right," replied Mr. Stevens, his smile vanishing as he thought of the military importance of this peaceful town, and again recalled the rumors that the Confederate Army, now, in the spring of 1863, at the high tide of their military success, were considering an invasion of Pennsylvania; and if such an invasion of a loyal state was carried out what town could offer such a centre as Gettysburg?

But he said nothing of these anxious thoughts to Kathleen, whose glance was now turned toward the ridge at the west of the town where the white cupola of the seminary rose clearly against the blue April sky.

The house of her Aunt Melvina Stevens was not far from the seminary, and Miss Stevens had promised Kathleen that she would some day take her to the cupola, telling the little girl that from that place one could look for miles in every direction; and Kathleen now wondered if it might not be possible that they would this very day climb up the stairs and look off toward South Mountain, the distant village of Cashtown, and down the wide turnpikes leading into Maryland. Kathleen resolved to remind Aunt

Melvina of her promise; it would be something to tell Mother and Ted, she thought, when she should be home again; and, occupied with pleasant thoughts of all the possibilities of her birthday visit, Kathleen did not notice her father's silence, and when they came in sight of the square stone house near the slope leading to the top of the ridge she called out:

"Father, look! Aunt Melvina has the flag up because it is my birthday," and Kathleen pointed to the "Stars and Stripes" waving over her aunt's house with the feeling that her birthday celebration was now really beginning.

The Stevens house was built of field stone, with a big chimney at each end. It had little windows in the roof, that always made Kathleen think of watchful eyes. It stood quite near the road, but a stone wall, over which grew a tangle of vines and rose-bushes, separated it from the street, and inside the wall there were beds of tall yellow daffodils, now in full blossom, and lilac trees budded for bloom; honeysuckle climbed the rough walls of the house, and woodbine and clematis trailed over the narrow porch.

Mr. Webb had not reached the gate when a woman came running down the foot-path calling a gay welcome; and Kathleen thought, as she often did when she saw her Aunt Melvina, that she did not "look like an aunt; she looks like a grown-up girl," and indeed Miss Melvina Stevens, with her pleasant grey eyes, her smooth brown hair, and her cheerful readiness to smile whenever children happened to glance her way, was, in spite of her thirty years, only a grown-up girl. She was Mrs. Webb's youngest sister, and lived in the family home. Her two brothers, Kathleen's uncles, for whom she kept house, were with the Union Army, so now Miss Melvina lived alone with two elderly servants.

"Aunty Mel! Aunty Mel!" called Kathleen. "I've brought you a rug! I made it myself! It's a surprise!" and the little girl ran to meet her aunt who exclaimed:

"Oh, you really are growing up," as she kissed the little girl, six times on each cheek, saying gaily: "One kiss a year for luck, and an extra for pluck!" and added quickly: "And where is the rug? I can hardly wait to see it."

"Father is bringing it," replied Kathleen, as Mr. Webb came up the path carrying a long, neatly wrapped package, which contained the "hooked" rug that Kathleen had made during the past winter.

As soon as they were indoors Miss Melvina untied the cords and spread the rug on the painted floor of the tiny front entry.

"It's a beauty!" she exclaimed.

"And I drew the pattern myself," declared Kathleen. "See, Aunty Mel, 'tis a rose-bush in the centre, and the vine goes to each corner. I drew it with a bit of charcoal, and I helped Mother fasten the burlap in the rug frame, and I did all the rest myself."

It was small wonder the little girl was proud of her handiwork: the groundwork of the rug was a soft leaf green, the roses were a pale creamy yellow, while the vine was a deep green. The surface of the rug was smooth and even, and it was made of bits of woolen cloth, cut in tiny shreds, and then drawn through the loosely woven burlap. As her father had said, it was Grandma Webb who had first taught her little granddaughter how to "hook" a rug, when Kathleen was very small indeed.

"That's a Yankee rug!" Mr. Webb declared smilingly, but Melvina shook her head.

"Pennsylvania women can make them," she said.

"Well, Pennsylvanians are Yankees now, you know," said Mr. Webb, as he followed Melvina and Kathleen into a square room at the end of the hall, and exclaimed approvingly: "Coffee! And waffles!" as a stout elderly negro woman came bustling into the room and set her tray on the table.

"And honey!" Melvina added, as she untied the broad white ribbon strings of Kathleen's pretty straw hat, and they all seated themselves at the round table in the centre of the room while Mammy Dosia, who had smilingly greeted Kathleen and Mr. Webb, turned out the fragrant coffee, and helped them to the hot waffles.

"I must start home at once," said Mr. Webb, as he finished his plate of waffles. "I promised Ted to help him with the wheat; the lad is a good farmer for a boy of fifteen, but he's getting uneasy, wants to be a soldier."

"All Pennsylvania boys now want to be soldiers, especially those whose fathers have fought," said Melvina, for Mr. Webb had been wounded at Bull Run, and even now limped a little, although he often declared himself as well as ever.

While her father and aunt talked of Ted, of the possibility that General Robert E. Lee might lead that army that seemed so unconquerable into Pennsylvania, Kathleen wandered about the sunny room, and on a table in the corner she noticed a small package. It was wrapped in white paper and tied with a pale blue cord. "That's for me! I'm sure it is. It's my birthday present! Oh, why doesn't Aunty Mel give it to me?" she thought, and suddenly it occurred to her that it would be a splendid joke on Aunt Mel to slip the little package into the pocket of her blue thibet skirt and say nothing about it. "Then when Aunty is ready to give it to me she'll find it's gone! And then

I'll say: 'Oh! Have you lost something?'" and
Kathleen found it difficult not to laugh aloud as,
with a quick glance toward her aunt who was now
near the door, Kathleen quickly slipped the package
into her pocket.

"Well, good-bye, Kathleen. Your aunt will bring
you home this afternoon, and maybe you will find a
'surprise' at home," called her father, and Kathleen
ran down to the gate to watch him drive away.

"Now, my dear, come and see your present," said
Aunt Mel, putting her arm about Kathleen's shoulders, and adding, "Oh, dear! your hair is growing
darker! It's almost copper color."

"Never mind," laughed Kathleen, shaking back
her mass of wavy hair, and wishing, as she so often
did, that her mother would permit her to have it cut
short. "Never mind my hair. I want to see my present," and she wondered why Aunty Mel led her along
the path toward the stable and barns instead of into
the house.

"Have you got to speak to Uncle Job?" she asked,
seeing the old negro man coming toward them; but
before Miss Melvina could reply Kathleen's glance
had discovered a stout brown pony harnessed to a little brown cart with a high-backed seat. It was just
such a pony and just such a cart, she thought, as any
girl would like; and she wondered what little

Gettysburg girl had driven out that morning to see Aunt Mel, who was leading Kathleen directly toward the brown pony.

"Here, 'Frisk'! Look up; this is your little mistress. Kathleen," and Miss Mel handed the white leather reins to her niece, "here is your birthday present."

CHAPTER II

THE MISSING BOX

FOR a moment Kathleen did not speak; she looked at the pony, at the reins in her hands, and then at Aunt Melvina who was smiling as if it were she who had just received the most wonderful present that anyone could possibly imagine; and then Kathleen realized that her dearest wish was fulfilled—that this fat, sleek brown pony m his shining harness, this pretty cart with its high-backed seat, was really her very own; and she dropped the white reins and flung her arms about her aunt exclaiming:

"Aunty Mel! Nobody thinks of such lovely things as you do! Oh! I never expected I would really ever have a pony;" and, although Kathleen had not really said "Thank you" her aunt seemed very well pleased.

"Suppose you take me for a drive," suggested Miss Melvina. "'Frisk' has not been exercised this morning, and I'd like to be the first who drives with you."

"Where will we go?" asked Kathleen, as she took her seat beside her aunt, and Uncle Job turned the pony's head toward the road and handed Kathleen the white reins.

"We might drive to Oak Ridge," suggested Miss Melvina, and Kathleen, who had often driven when riding with her father or Ted, now guided "Frisk" along the smooth turnpike leading to Oak Ridge where the seminary buildings could be clearly seen. "Frisk" trotted along at a good pace as if he enjoyed the warm spring air, the fragrance of ploughed fields and budding flowers, as much as did Miss Mel and Kathleen. Kathleen's "copper-colored" hair blew back from her face, her blue eyes shone with happiness, and her cheeks were flushed with the pleasure of the possession of "Frisk." Miss Mel's face glowed with satisfaction as she looked at her little niece and told herself that Kathleen was surely the dearest and prettiest girl in all Pennsylvania.

"Are we going straight to the seminary, Aunt Mel?" asked Kathleen, as the road turned along the summit of the ridge.

"Why not? Would you not like to go up to the cupola and look off toward South Mountain, and, for that matter, all over Gettysburg?" said Miss Mel. "And I think it is as far as we ought to drive without our hats, even if it is as warm as summer."

Kathleen promptly agreed. She would have liked to drive "Frisk" on and on; but it had long been one of her cherished wishes to climb to the top of this large building and see the view of which her mother had often told her, and she brought the pony to a standstill in the pleasant shade of a wide-spreading oak tree where a stretch of grass ground bordered the highway.

"This is a good place to leave him, isn't it, Aunt Mel?" she asked, and Miss Melvina declared that no place could be better, and showed Kathleen how to fasten the pony's bridle rein to a convenient fence pole close at hand, and in a few moments they had reached the entrance to the seminary and were climbing the stairs toward the cupola.

"Everything splendid is happening to me to-day!" Kathleen declared. "First and best, is my pony; but here am I almost at the top of the seminary, and——" But Kathleen suddenly stopped, for they had reached the cupola, and there spread out before them like a beautiful picture lay the peaceful town of Gettysburg, with its gardens and shade trees and comfortable homes. Looking over the tree tops rose the South Mountain range, and nearer at hand Kathleen's eyes rested on a high granite spur that rose above the dense growth of oaks and pines. This granite spur was called Little Round Top, and Kathleen now remembered that Ted had climbed it only the previous week.

A soft haze hung over the distant mountains, and the delicate greens of the young beech leaves, the deeper green of the dark pines, and here and there the silvery stems of a group of birches made up a picture that Kathleen always recalled when she thought of Gettysburg.

"I can see all the 'spokes of the wheel,'" she said, and told Miss Mel of Ted's declaring that Gettysburg was the hub and the eleven roads that centered in the town were the spokes of a big wheel.

"Yes; and I hope the Southern Army may not realize that we are but seven miles from Maryland with the best roads in the country," responded Miss Melvina, for the moment forgetting that her companion was a little girl celebrating her eleventh birthday.

But at the mention of the Southern Army Kathleen's glance came back from the distant pink of a peach orchard in a field toward Round Top, and she asked eagerly: "Would General Robert E. Lee come with the Southern Army if they invaded Pennsylvania?"

"Why, Kathleen! You sound as if you thought it would be a fine thing for Gettysburg for General Lee and his army to come marching upon us. And you a Yankee girl!" said Miss Mel, smiling at Kathleen's sober face; "but General Lee would surely come with his army, my dear. But we must hope he will be satisfied with his Virginia victories and not bring the war into Pennsylvania."

"Aunty Mel, I wish I could see General Lee! My father says he is the finest man in all the South," said Kathleen.

"Well, listen to that! and your father a Yankee soldier!" said her aunt. "But I hope you will not see the splendid Lee at present, dear child," and Miss Mel's face once more grew serious, as she looked off to the misty range of South Mountain.

Kathleen again turned her glance toward the peach orchard, but at that moment she made the resolve—a resolve that before the summer ended was to bring her into great peril. "If General Lee does come to Gettysburg I'll see him," Kathleen told herself, not realizing that the invasion of Southern armies would mean a terrible battle, and perhaps the defeat of the Northern forces.

" Mustn't keep 'Frisk' waiting too long," said Aunt Mel, as she clasped Kathleen by the hand and drew the little girl toward the stairway. "And there's another birthday 'surprise,'" she added, and at this Kathleen suddenly remembered the little package that she had taken from the table and that was now safe in her own pocket, and for a moment she was tempted to draw it out and tell her aunt of the "joke" she had planned, but Aunty Mel was again speaking: "I think I must tell you that the next 'surprise' is company for your birthday dinner."

"Oh, Aunty Mel! Is it Beth and Janet?" Kathleen asked eagerly, and at her aunt's smiling nod she exclaimed happily: "Oh! Everything lovely is happening to-day! I do wish every day was a birthday!"

"But you'd be a hundred years old before you knew it," laughed Miss Mel, as she took her seat beside the happy girl who now urged the pony to its fastest pace toward home, thinking to herself that Beth and Janet were sure to admire "Frisk," and resolving to let each one of them drive the pony at some future day.

Beth and Janet Ross were twin sisters who lived not far from the Stevens farm. Unlike most twins they did not look much alike, for Beth was fat and Janet thin. They had just passed their tenth birthday, and they were the only little girls that Kathleen knew well enough to think of as real friends; and now, as she turned "Frisk" into the driveway that led to the stable, Kathleen remembered that Beth and Janet were not as fortunate as she knew herself to be: their father had been killed at Bull Run, and their mother was doing her best to make the farm give her family a comfortable livelihood, but there was no extra money to be used to give Beth and Janet the pretty hats, dresses and many pleasures that Kathleen's parents could so easily give her; and something of all this flashed through Kathleen's thoughts, as she patted "Frisk's" brown head, and then followed her aunt indoors.

Dosia came hurrying to say that "De company's in de fore room," and Kathleen ran forward to greet the two girls who stood in the open doorway smiling, a little soberly it seemed to the happy Kathleen, as they called out: "Happy birthday!" and Beth handed her a package saying: "We made it for you, Kathleen!" and Kathleen thanked them earnestly, thinking she would ask her mother to invite Beth and Janet to visit at the Webb farm, and then Janet said: "Why don't you look at our present, Kathleen?" and they all laughed because Kathleen was holding the square package as carefully as if it were glass.

She took off the paper in which it was wrapped, and exclaimed with admiring pleasure at the pretty box. At the first glance it looked to be the cone of a pine tree, but Kathleen was quick to see that it was made of wood, with the small petals of pine cones cleverly fastened on, one overlapping the other, in the same fashion as on a pine cone.

"Mother showed us how to make it," Janet explained, as she lifted the pointed end of the cone-shaped box. "Beth made the wooden part from a piece of old cedar. See, Kathleen, she cut out the center bit by bit with a sharp knife, and then made the cover. Is it not smooth?" and Janet regarded the inside of the box admiringly.

"But 'twas Janet stuck on the cone petals. Mother told her how to do it, with hot mucilage," Beth explained. "We thought you could keep your locket and chain and your pearl beads in it," she added, a little questioningly, so that Kathleen quickly responded that the cone box would be exactly right to hold such treasures, and again thanked the twins for making it for her.

"I'll always keep it," she promised," and when I go back to Maine I'll have it to remember you by."

"But you are not going back to Maine, are you, Kathleen?" Beth questioned anxiously. "I thought your father and mother were going to live here always."

"Oh, I guess we'll go back sometime," said Kathleen, who often made plans for a "surprise visit" to Grandpa and Grandma Webb.

The twins had seen "Frisk" on his arrival on the previous day, and were quite ready to agree with Kathleen that he was all a pony could possibly be in beauty, good temper and swiftness.

"I mean to ride horseback," said Kathleen. "I know Father will get me a saddle, and when you come to visit me you shall both ride," and the twins happily declared that they hoped they could soon visit the Webb farm.

Miss Melvina had left the little girls by themselves, but she now came to call them to dinner, and the little girls followed her into the pleasant room where Kathleen and her father had eaten waffles only a few hours earlier.

It was a real birthday dinner, with roast duckling, and jelly, with sweet potatoes and corn pancakes, and slender glasses filled with grape-juice. And then the door into the kitchen opened and in came the smiling Dosia holding up a round blue plate, and on the plate stood a cake! A cake covered with heavy white frosting; and right across the top of the cake in heavy pink sugar letters was the word "Kathleen," and just below it the figure "11."

Kathleen stood up to cut the cake with the wide bladed silver knife that Dosia handed her; and in Janet's piece there was a finely chased gold ring; Beth's piece held a pretty silver thimble, while Miss Mel found a shoe-button in her cake, and Kathleen had nothing at all.

Kathleen was just thinking that she would give the other half of the big cake to Beth and Janet to take home to their mother; when her aunt said:

"Dosia, there is a little package on the corner table; please bring it to me." Then, with a smile at her young guests, she added, "This isn't another present for Kathleen; it is something for you, my dears," and she nodded toward Beth and Janet.

"Dar ain' no package whatsumever on dis table," declared Dosia. And as she spoke Kathleen reached into her pocket, meaning to draw out the box and say: "Here it is, Aunt Mel." Her hand went down and down, and there was no box there!

"Aunty Mel!" she exclaimed aloud and in another moment would have told of the joke she had planned and that now the box was lost, had not Miss Mel jumped up from the table saying: "Why, it must be there! I put it there myself just as Kathleen arrived this morning. I am sure no one would touch it," and she hurried to the table to make sure that Dosia had not overlooked it; and now Kathleen felt that she could not tell her aunt that she had taken the present intended for Beth and Janet and lost it.

"I must find the box, then I'll tell her," she decided, as Miss Mel at last acknowledged that Dosia was right, that there was no box on the table.

"I'll run up-stairs and look on my table," she said with another smile at Beth and Janet, who were looking at each other in such evident disappointment that Kathleen felt more guilty than before, and without a word ran out of the room toward the stable-yard, for she had suddenly thought perhaps the box might have dropped on the floor of the pony-cart.

CHAPTER III

PAYING A DEBT

THE box was not to be found, and when Kathleen again examined her pocket she found a hole through which the package could easily have slipped. She was back in the dining-room before her aunt came downstairs, and Beth and Janet, somewhat to Kathleen's surprise, did not seem greatly disappointed by the disappearance of the present intended for them.

"Do you think your mother would let you both make me a visit?" Kathleen asked, thinking to herself that she must find out what had been in the package and try and give Beth and Janet something exactly like it.

"Perhaps so," Beth responded. "When would you like to have us come?"

"I'd like to have you come for May day and stay all night!" declared Kathleen. "You ask your mother and let me know!"

"Let's go ask her now, and you come with us; it won't take a minute!" suggested Janet eagerly, and a moment later Miss Melvina looked from her window to see the three little girls racing down the road.

"We never went on a visit in all our life," said Janet as they reached the Ross's cottage, and where Mrs. Ross listened smilingly to Kathleen's request that Bath and Janet might come out to the Webb farm for a May day visit.

"Ted and I will come after them," Kathleen promised, and Mrs. Ross said the twins could go, and seemed nearly as pleased as did the little girls themselves; and as Kathleen and her friends ran back to Miss Melvina's they began making plans for all they would do when May day came, and Kathleen almost forgot that she was to blame for the lost package; and when Aunty Mel soberly announced that the box could not be found she exclaimed: "Never mind! I'm going to plan a present for Beth and Janet," and wondered why Aunty Mel should smile so approvingly.

The two weeks between Kathleen's birthday and the day set for her friends' visit passed quickly. She now rode "Frisk" about the paths and roads near the farm, and had twice driven her mother into Gettysburg. It had been decided, however, that Miss Melvina would bring Janet and Beth to the farm, and on the day set for their arrival Kathleen was unusually busy. As soon as she had eaten her breakfast she had run up-stairs and looked into the room where Beth and Janet were to sleep. It was just across a narrow passageway from Kathleen's room, and its windows looked out over pleasant fields and orchards toward Rock Creek. Kathleen gave a little exclamation of delight as she stood in the doorway and her glance rested on the two beds; but it was not the smooth beds with their tufted spreads and lace-trimmed pillows, nor the ruffled muslin curtains at the windows, the shining pumpkin yellow of the painted floor with its pretty home-made rugs, or any of the furnishings of the chamber over which she exclaimed for, except for the extra bed, the room was very much like her own; but on each bed in this room rested a white muslin dress, "like white clouds," Kathleen told herself as she gazed admiringly at the fluffy lace trimmed skirts, and then at the wide ruffled sash resting beside each dress.

For these white dresses were Kathleen's May day present to her friends; her mother and aunt had been surprised by Kathleen's eagerness and insistence that it was really to be her gift to Beth and Janet, and Mrs. Webb had consented to Kathleen's emptying her tin bank to pay for the muslin; and beside that Kathleen had helped make the dresses. Each day sitting beside her mother she had hemmed ruffles and taken out basting-threads as if there were no better fun in all the world. And now as she looked at the pretty gowns she gave a little chuckle and told herself that, no matter what Aunt Mel had put in that lost package, it could not be prettier than these dresses.

"But I wish Aunty Mel would tell me what her present was just the same." Kathleen's thoughts were never quite comfortable thoughts about that lost package, but to-day, looking at her gift for the twins, she felt happier than she had since her birthday. From the beds her glance turned to the bureau where stood a blue bowl filled with wild trillium and ferns and violets that she had gathered the previous day; everything was ready to welcome her friends and Kathleen now ran back to the kitchen where her mother was busy helping Hitty, Mammy Dosia's daughter, who was just taking a cake from the oven and who looked over her shoulder to smile at Kathleen and say:

"I reckon yo' comp'ny nebber taste a better cake dan dis one! 'Leben eggs, poun' ob butter, poun' ob——" but Kathleen did not wait to hear the remainder of the list as she went over to the window where her mother with a big silver spoon was beating up a white frothy mixture which Kathleen knew was the frosting for the big cake.

"Mother, could you make letters out of sugar? Could you make a B. and a J.? Could you, Mother?" and she looked so anxiously into her mother's face that Mrs. Webb again wondered why Kathleen wanted to do so much for the little Ross girls; but she smiled and replied that she was quite sure she could make letters of sugar for the top of the cake.

"And will you, Mother dear? Will you? And may I not tell Beth and Janet that it is their own special cake? Aunt Mel says that Mrs. Ross cannot afford cakes!" she added, and Mrs. Webb did not need this knowledge to make her quite ready to promise that this particular cake should be what Kathleen called Beth and Janet's "special cake."

Having made sure of this Kathleen put on her wide-rimmed straw hat and ran off to the pasture where "Frisk" was quietly feeding, but he did not stop near the pony but kept on to the spring that bubbled up at the foot of a steep ledge, well out of sight of the house. Tall ferns grew just above it, and near by a bed of white violets flourished, and as the little girl knelt and began to pick the delicate blossoms a brown partridge whirred up, and, dragging a wing as if it were broken, staggered clumsily into the underbrush.

"I know all about *you*," Kathleen called. "You are just making believe so I won't find your young chicks! Oh, here they come!" and a dozen little round partridge chicks came huddling together to vanish at the point where the mother partridge had disappeared.

Sitting back on her heels Kathleen looked up at the steep ledge, and then toward the thick growth of pine trees that stretched toward the brook, and smiled happily as she thought of the two May baskets that she had made on the previous day and that she meant to hang on the chamberdoor for Beth and Janet.

She had made the baskets of strips of birch bark cleverly plaited together, with handles of pliant young willow twigs. The baskets were to be filled with feathery green moss that grew in one of the crevices of the ledge not far from the spring, and with white violets.

"I ought to write a verse for each basket," she told herself, "something about how glad I am that they are here for May day," and now various rhymes began to sing through Kathleen's thoughts as she climbed the ledge to the mossy crevice where she had left her May baskets, and proceeded to fill them with the damp moss and flowers.

She had been there only a few moments when the sound of voices close at hand made her look quickly about; but she was so shut in by the ledge on one side and by a growth of dogwoods on the other that she could not see, or be seen, by anyone; and she did not recognize the voice that was speaking:

"I tell you Gettysburg is as easily to be captured as if it had been planned for the Southern Army to take it. And from here Lee can move on to Washington, Baltimore, even to Philadelphia; in a word, conquer the Northern Army on their own soil."

Kathleen held her breath as she listened eagerly for the response.

"Don't speak so loud; there's a house not far off, and some workman or child may be near," she heard, and then the first voice responded:

"No fear of that; this ledge is straight up and down on the sides toward the farm. I reckon General Lee has his plans to make a big move before long, perhaps to Harrisburg; his army is ready for anything, while the Yanks have been beaten so many times they have lost courage."

"Don't be too sure of that," came the quick response. "General Hooker is brave enough, and with Hancock and Meade at hand the fight might not be too easy. But we'd best be moving on. I have a plan of all the General will need to know about this part of the country," and Kathleen heard a scrambling movement toward the top of the ledge and knew that the men were gone.

"Lee's scouts," the little girl whispered to herself, forgetting her May baskets and that Janet and Beth Ross were probably now on their way for the long expected visit. For in the spring of 1863 children as well as their elders knew how serious and terrible was the conflict that was to determine whether the United States should remain an undivided nation, as the North believed right, or be rent in twain as the South believed feasible; and beyond this: if Lee and his armies continued their triumphs the slavery of the negroes might continue, while if the Northern armies won the blacks could no longer be bought and sold.

Something of all this flashed through Kathleen's thoughts as, leaving her baskets behind her, she crept noiselessly toward the spring where for a moment she stood perfectly still listening. But there was no unfamiliar sound, and the little girl realized that the men who had stopped to rest among the rocks and bushes of the ledge were now out of sight in the thick growths of tall pines that stretched off toward the Maryland border line.

"I must tell my father," she decided, and ran swiftly across the pastures toward the field where her father and Ted were at work.

Mr. Webb's face grew anxious as he listened to Kathleen's breathless story of the conversation she had overheard, and Ted was eager to start off at once and endeavor to capture the Confederate scouts, but at this suggestion Mr. Webb shook his head.

"It couldn't be done. The men are miles away before this; but it is fortunate Kathleen overheard what she did. I'll let the men of Gettysburg know what's being talked of so freely and that there is no doubt that General Lee means to bring the seat of war into Pennsylvania."

Kathleen listened to every word. If this great General of the Southern forces, a man beloved by his own men and deeply respected by his Northern opponents, really came near her home perhaps, she thought hopefully, she might see him. The terrible results of such an invasion she could not even imagine, and when she turned toward home Kathleen pictured to herself a fine soldierly man who would smile upon her in a friendly way; and that, indeed, was exactly what General Lee was to do before Kathleen's next birthday.

Miss Melvina with Bath and Janet Ross reached the Webb farm early in the afternoon, but Mrs. Webb had cautioned Kathleen not to mention her morning's adventure, and nothing was said of the menace of advancing armies that might soon sweep over this peaceful countryside; and in the excitement of welcoming Beth and Janet, who had never before visited her, Kathleen forgot for the time her father's anxiety and her own wish to see General Robert Lee, and was eager to lead Beth and Janet to the front chamber and hear what they would have to say to the pretty white muslin dresses.

Kathleen was quick to notice that the dresses worn by the twins were faded from a former blue to a dull white, and that their well-polished shoes had been mended, and their hats were the same ones they had worn all winter; but neither Beth nor Janet seemed to be thinking about what they wore; they were evidently bubbling over with delight at the fact that they were really at the beginning of the promised visit, and they accepted the muslin dresses with so much admiration that Kathleen jumped about the room as if she were a frisky kitten instead of a girl eleven years old, and it was not until nearly suppertime that the least shadow fell upon her pleasure. The three little girls were all talking happily together of the May day picnic planned for the coming day, when Beth exclaimed:

"Oh, Kathleen! We know now what was in the little box that was lost on your birthday, the box Miss Mel was going to give to Janet and me!"

Kathleen waited; she could not even ask what that lost package held, but instantly Beth went on: "You never could guess, and Miss Mel doesn't know that we know; but we do. Dosia told us. Kathleen! Just think, there were two five dollar gold pieces in that box; one for Janet and one for me. Isn't it too bad they were lost!" and Kathleen's exclamation convinced the twins that she was as sorry about it as they could possibly be.

CHAPTER IV

VISITORS

KATHLEEN did her best not to let Beth and Janet see that she was more sorry than they could possibly be about the lost box; and she told herself that being sorry was not enough; if she could not find that box then she must see to it that Beth and Janet each received a five dollar gold piece; and as glancing toward her friends she again noticed how worn and shabby their dresses and shoes were, Kathleen found it a little difficult to swallow comfortably as she realized that the lost gold pieces would have bought new shoes and hats for both Janet and Beth.

But how ever could she find an excuse to go searching for the missing box to the cupola of the seminary, where, she began to feel sure, it must have fallen from her pocket? And if it was not to be found how ever could a little girl earn ten dollars?

"Rugs!" Kathleen suddenly exclaimed so that Beth and Janet stared at her in amazement and Kathleen quickly added: "Come and see the rug I am making," and hurried them through the sitting-room to a long narrow room whose windows looked out toward the meadows and ledge and distant forest.

This room was Kathleen's schoolroom, workroom and playhouse, and Beth's round face beamed with interest as she glanced from the book-shelves to a big globe of the world, while Janet's hazel eyes shone with pleasure as she discovered the frame holding the burlap foundation for the rug Kathleen was at work on.

"Isn't it splendid to go to school at home? I wish we could," said Beth, resting both hands on the low solid table on which stood the frame holding the globe.

"Oh, Beth! Think of all the fun we have at recess with the other girls! And singing, too! And even staying after school when Miss Smith talks to us in fun!" Janet eagerly declared; but Beth shook her curly head in disagreement, and Kathleen for the time forgot to be troubled about how she could replace the lost gold pieces. She helped Beth discover Africa on the globe, and China and Japan, and pointed out New England, where her Grandma Webb lived; and, in answer to Beth's eager questions, told them just how she "went to school at home."

"Mother and I read stories about history," she said, "about little girls in far-off times who knew kings and queens and brave soldiers. And I learn a poem every week, and I draw pictures, and Ted and I work out games out of an arithmetic."

"Arithmetic isn't a game; it's addition and subtraction and multiplication and division and fractions!" declared Beth; but Kathleen laughed delightedly.

"It's games, just the same! Puzzles and games, that you work out with figures," she said, "and every day I write a letter to my Grandma Webb, but only send them once a week; and I go on journeys around the globe! That's fun! I start at Gettysburg and go to New York and take a steamer for Constantinople," and Kathleen pointed out on the globe some of her travels to the surprised twins and even Janet began to think that, after all, there was much to be said for the way Kathleen went to school.

They all gathered about the rug and admired its pattern. Kathleen had drawn a small pine tree in the center, and in each corner was a branch of pine; "and it is to be all green, different shades," she explained. "Hitty dyed a lot of pieces for me. And she said the rug would be worth five dollars. I could make two rugs and that would be ten dollars," she added thoughtfully.

"Who would you sell them to?" questioned Beth.

But before Kathleen could consider this puzzling question Hitty appeared in the doorway.

"Yo' supper all ready, Missie Kathie," she announced, and Kathleen's thoughts fled to the big "special" cake that was to surprise Beth and Janet, and she hurried the little girls to the dining-room where Aunty Mel, in a silvery grey gown, Mrs. Webb and Mr. Webb and Ted were all waiting for them. But it was Kathleen who was more surprised than Beth and Janet, and she exclaimed in delight as her glance rested first on the windows, that were wreathed with vines and dogwood blossoms, and then at the table which seemed to be set in a blossoming arbor; for Miss Melvina, Mrs. Webb and Ted had been at work ever since Miss Mel's arrival setting up a light framework, that Mr. Webb had made, and that enclosed the table; this framework was wreathed with branches of lilacs and dogwood blossoms and it was small wonder that Kathleen was sure that nothing could be more lovely than this supper table spread so abundantly.

Ted smilingly welcomed his sister's friends; and he looked so much like Kathleen that both Beth and Janet felt instantly acquainted with the tall boy who so politely drew their chairs back from the table for them.

Everyone enjoyed the excellent supper, and when the cake was brought in and Kathleen bade Beth and Janet tell her what the big pink sugar "B" and "J" stood for, and when the twins realized that it was their own special cake they smiled so radiantly that everyone else at the table smiled in response, and it seemed to Kathleen that her Aunt Mel looked toward her with even more approval than usual. But as they all left the table Aunt Mel put her arm about Kathleen and whispered: "I know why you are trying to do so much for Janet and Beth; it's because you are sorry about the lost box!" and Kathleen fairly gasped in astonishment and dismay, for she was sure her aunt must know that she had taken the box and lost it, but before she could stammer out that she had taken it in fun, Miss Mel's soft voice continued: "But I believe I'll find it yet. It must be in the house. Didn't you see it on the table?"

"Mel, come in the sitting-room," called Mrs. Webb, and without waiting for Kathleen's reply Miss Melvina hurried away, and Kathleen followed her brother and the twins out of doors, where Ted suggested that he should show the girls some "horseback tricks," and led his little grey horse out from the stable saying: "I have trained 'Patch' myself, and he knows every word I say; don't you, 'Patch'?" and the little horse, who was named because of the patches of black on his shoulders, bowed his head and whinnied in response. Then Ted sprang lightly to "Patch's" back, and without curb or bridle, balancing himself first on one foot and then on the other, sent the horse at a canter around the yard.

"I'm going to teach 'Frisk' all these things," declared Kathleen, after "Patch" at Ted's command had made a low bow and offered his right fore hoof to each little girl, and then trotted obediently off to graze.

"Oh, I guess not!" laughed Ted. "'Frisk' is too old to learn tricks; he's two years old, and I began to teach 'Patch' before he was three months old."

But Kathleen and Beth were both confident that it would be an easy matter to teach the pony to bow and offer his forefoot in greeting, and Beth was sure that she could ride standing on the pony's fat back, and Kathleen promised they would give the pony his first lesson on the following morning.

They were all turning back to the house when the sound of a galloping horse made them look toward the highway and Ted exclaimed: "That's a Union soldier. I can see the blue coat," and a moment later the horseman drew rein directly in front of the gate where the children were standing, and as Ted stepped forward he asked:

"Is this the best road to Gettysburg?"

"As good as any of the other, sir," Ted answered, hoping the stranger would ask him to explain more about the roads leading into Gettysburg; but Mr. Webb came hurrying toward the gate and urged the stranger to dismount and rest.

"We are celebrating May day eve, and supper has not been taken from the table. I am sure these little girls want you to taste a fine frosted cake," said Mr. Webb smilingly, as he told the stranger that his name was Webb, and that he had but recently finished his service with the Northern Army.

The soldier responded that his name was Mason, and that he would be glad of rest and refreshment; and as he walked toward the house with Mr. Webb Ted led the tired horse toward the stable.

Kathleen and the twins followed Mr. Webb and the soldier into the dining-room and the little girls smiled at each other at the stranger's exclamation of surprise and admiration over the flower-decked room. He was evidently very tired, and when Mrs. Webb came to welcome him and suggested that hot tea should be made for him, and added that Hitty could beat up and cook an omelette the young man declared that he was ashamed to make trouble then he was hungry enough to eat anything.

Kathleen ran to the kitchen to bring in a plate of freshly baked biscuit, while Beth and Janet seated themselves near one of the windows, where Kathleen soon joined them, and the three little girls whispered together over their May day plans until the soldier's story awoke their interest and they listened almost unconsciously. He was telling of his visit to his home in Philadelphia, and that he was now on his way to join the Army of the Potomac that was, in May, 1863, resting on one side of the Rappahannock River, while on the southern side of the river the Confederate Army of Northern Virginia, behind a strong line of earthworks, was apparently idle while in reality preparing for a tremendous effort against its enemy.

The young soldier declared that Lee had a force of seventy thousand men, "Men of the finest quality who have proved their mettle, and commanded by the finest of officers," he added, and Mr. Webb agreed; for although the North had entered war to defend the integrity of the Union, the supremacy of the Constitution, and to set free the negroes, and while Mr. Webb had himself fought in the Northern Army, he realized the nobility of the Southern men who were equally sure of their right to divide the nation into a Northern and a Southern Republic. On each side was perfect faith in their leaders, and in the justice of their cause.

Mr. Webb told his visitor of Kathleen's adventure that morning when the little girl had overheard the conversation of the Confederate scouts as they rested on the ledge, and the young soldier was evidently greatly interested and asked Kathleen to repeat exactly what the men had said, and as he listened his face grew a little troubled.

"I am sure this news is valuable, of great importance," he declared, "and I mean it shall reach head-quarters as soon as possible," and as he spoke the young soldier rose to his feet, thanking Mr. and Mrs. Webb for their hospitality as he moved toward the door; but just before leaving the room he turned and held out his hand to Kathleen saying:

"I wish I had been the one to hear those scouts declare that Lee meant to enter Pennsylvania. I'd like to tell General Buford of capturing them; but you may be sure he shall hear that a little Gettysburg girl told me."

"And do you think General Lee will really come here?" questioned Kathleen, and at the soldier's answer: "Do not be afraid; if Lee comes the Union Army will be here to meet him," Kathleen's smile vanished, and Mr. Webb, resting his hand on his little daughter's arm, said:

"My little girl cannot realize what a terrible misfortune it would be for Lee to invade Pennsylvania; she thinks of him as a wonderful soldier, a fine hero, riding at the head of a wonderful army."

"Well, he is all that," declared the young Union officer. "Nevertheless I hope he'll keep out of Pennsylvania."

They all stood at the gate to watch the young soldier ride away. The spring twilight was deepening into darkness as they turned back to the house, and the older members of the party grew silent as they realized the possibility that before the summer ended terrible warfare might enter their state; but none of them could even dream that the hills and fields of Gettysburg were to be the scene of a conflict that would give the name historic immortality.

Kathleen, thinking of her May baskets among the ferns at the foot of the ledge, resolved to be up at an early hour to fetch them to hang on the door of the twins' room so they would discover them the first thing on May day morning. She decided that she would write the verses for the baskets before going to bed. Beth did not notice the silence of her companions, for a plan was taking form in her thoughts; she was deciding that she would get up the next morning before anyone else in the house. For she had resolved to go to the pasture and practice riding "Frisk" as she had seen Ted ride "Patch."

"I may never have another chance," thought Beth, "and there's no harm in riding 'Frisk'; Kathleen said we could, but I'd rather ride without anybody seeing me the first time; then when she sees how well I ride standing up on the pony's back I guess she'll be s'prised, and then I'll tell her about getting up early to practice."

Absorbed in their plans neither Kathleen nor Beth noticed that Janet was smiling to herself as she walked slowly on beside them, smiling as if she were thinking of something very pleasant indeed, as she was, in fact, for Janet as well as Kathleen and Beth had made a plan for early rising on May day morning; and it was Janet's plan, as it proved, that was to seriously surprise Ted and interfere with his most cherished scheme.

CHAPTER V

MAY DAY

KATHLEEN was very well pleased with the verses that she finally wrote neatly out on small squares of paper which she meant to fasten to the May baskets. On one paper she wrote: "To Janet Ross," and directly beneath it were these lines:

> "Here is a basket for Janet;
>   The prettiest one that I've made yet.
> With it I send
> The best of good wishes
> From your true friend."

Under Beth's name she had written:

> "May day flowers and wishes, too;
>   The best of everything I wish you.
> May all Beth's May days happy be
> And every one be spent with me."

"It would be splendid if I could only put a five dollar gold piece in each basket," Kathleen thought, a little mournfully, as she remembered how long it would take to make two hooked rugs; for to make rugs and find a purchaser now seemed the only way she could ever earn the money to replace that in the lost box. More than once had Kathleen firmly resolved to tell Aunt Mel exactly what had happened; but, although she was sure that her aunt would have understood if her little niece had told her the moment the loss of the box was discovered, so long a time had now passed that Kathleen no longer thought of telling until she could either find the box, or have two bright gold pieces for the Ross twins. "Then I'd tell about it," she would promise herself, for she knew she would feel troubled until she had told Aunt Mel.

Before she went to sleep she made the resolve to do her best to persuade her mother to let her go home with Aunt Mel on the following afternoon; for once within driving distance of the seminary, thought Kathleen, it would be an easy matter to search for the box.

"And maybe I'll find it," thought the little girl, and went to sleep without even a thought of armies, scouts or soldiers, or of the possibility of General Robert E. Lee's appearance in Gettysburg.

When Beth awoke on May day morning the tall clock that stood in the front hallway was striking

five, and the spring sunshine filled the room. In a
moment the little girl was out of bed, and turned
anxiously to make sure that she had not awakened
Janet; but as Beth's glance rested on her sister's bed
she exclaimed in surprise: "Where is she?" for Janet
was not to be seen.

"Oh, I'll bet she and Kathleen have a secret,"
thought the puzzled girl. "Perhaps it's May baskets,
or perhaps they're teaching 'Frisk'!" And, wishing
that she might have awakened at an earlier hour,
Beth dressed hurriedly and crept down the stairs to
find the front door wide open, and as she ran along
the path behind the tall lilac bushes she could hear
Aunt Hitty vigorously at work in the kitchen.

"Oh, dear! It isn't so early after all," she thought,
looking toward the stable yard a little anxiously.
But there was no one to be seen there. Beth could
not know that early as it seemed to her the cows
had already been milked and turned into the meadows to graze.

She ran toward the pasture beyond the stable
where yesterday she had seen the pony, but he was
not there, and Beth now cautiously ventured into the
stable and instantly the pony's welcoming whinny
and his brown head stretching out over the door of
his roomy stall gave the little girl a sense of security,

and she ran toward him and stroked his head and fed him the bits of sugar that she had last night taken from the supper table for this very purpose.

"Frisk" seemed as well pleased to see his visitor as Beth had been to discover him, and was evidently eager to get out in the sunshine.

"Yes, 'Frisk,' just wait a minute and I'll let you out," Beth promised, and after a quick glance to make sure that no one was coming toward the stable she reached up and drew back the stout bar that held the stall door and pulled it open.

"Come out, 'Frisk,'" she said, quite expecting the pony to walk quietly out and wait for her to grasp his mane and lead him wherever she wanted him to go, so that when "Frisk" darted out, kicking up his heels in delight at his freedom, the surprised girl stepped backward and stumbling over an empty bucket found herself lying on her back on the stable floor, while "Frisk" raced about the stable yard, and there being no one to interfere, decided he would take a run down the road; so off he went, and by the time Beth had scrambled to her feet and reached the yard "Frisk" was dashing along the highway, and Beth, frightened and surprised, fled after him calling:

"'Frisk!' 'Frisk!' Oh, I must catch him!"

Beth could not run very fast, but she did her best and managed to keep in sight of the brown pony until a turn in the road hid him from view. But this did not alarm her until reaching the curve she looked along the grey stretch of highway and realized there was no brown pony in sight.

"He's resting!" Beth told herself, and no longer ran at her best speed but walked hopefully on looking from side to side of the wide roadway, expecting to discover "Frisk" feeding contentedly. How she was to capture or control the pony after finding him did not even occur to Beth as she trudged sturdily on, and she had quite forgotten to wonder what had become of Janet.

It was Janet who was the earliest riser at the Webb farm on that May day morning. She was awake a full hour before Beth, and had dressed and left the house so quietly that no one had heard her. Janet's secret plan was not unlike her sister's; for Janet had resolved to take her first riding lesson without anyone looking on; only she decided it would be easier to ride "Patch," as the little grey horse seemed so friendly and quiet; and after riding "Patch," thought Janet, it would be a surprise to Kathleen and Beth to see how easily she could ride the pony. It did not occur to either of the twins that there was any possible harm in the plan that each, unknown to the other, had made; and as Janet ran along over the grassy path behind the lilac bushes she was smiling happily over the success of her plan and nearly ran against the little grey horse that, saddled and bridled with an army knapsack fastened to his saddle-bow, stood so quietly hidden behind the close-growing bushes.

"My gracious sakes!" exclaimed the surprised girl, looking quickly about, quite sure that Ted must be close at hand. But there was no one near; the early morning was cool and shadowy, and Janet shivered a little in her cotton frock. She patted the grey horse, and now the thought that someone had meant to steal "Patch" occurred to her. "Maybe I frightened them away," she decided hopefully, and promptly decided that it would not do to let "Patch" remain hidden behind the lilacs, and discovering that he was secured by his bridle-rein she untied it, and led the well-trained horse down the little slope toward a big stump that, thought Janet, was just right to stand on and then mount "Patch"; and this she found proved as easy as she had expected, and she settled herself on the saddle, gathered up the reins and laughed aloud, thinking that there could be nothing more splendid than to be mounted on

"Patch" and have the whole world to herself. In her satisfaction Janet kicked her heels sharply against the horse's sides, and to "Patch" those kicks had a definite meaning: he had been taught that two sharp kicks meant "jump!" and as there was a low stone wall, bordering the highway, just in front of him, "Patch" cleared it at a bound and feeling the reins tighten, as Janet clutched them frantically, he went off at a great pace, and when Ted called from the field, as the astonished boy rushed angrily down the slope in pursuit, it was too late for "Patch" or Janet to hear, for the grey horse was racing along the highway and the frightened Janet had dropped the reins and was clinging to mane and saddle in order to keep on his back.

"It's one of those girls!" muttered Ted, running after his horse. "I hope she'll stick on. The little fool! What is she up and out for at this hour? Some May day trick, I suppose," and Ted forgot for a moment that very likely this unexpected happening might defeat his plan for joining the Union Army. For after the departure of their soldier guest the boy had made up his mind to run away. The soldier had said that the Northern Army needed more troops, that it had been defeated in a number of important battles and its men were losing courage, and Ted, feeling himself nearly a man, sixteen that very month, felt as did so many boys in 1863, boys of the South and boys of the North, that they wanted to fight for the right; and to Ted Webb of Gettysburg, Pennsylvania, the right meant the freedom of the negroes, and an undivided nation, to be won only by the success of the Northern Army, and Ted had packed a few belongings in his father's knapsack before he went to bed, and this morning had crept out while it was yet dark, saddled "Patch," and, had Janet only slept a half-hour longer, the boy would have made a good start and possibly carried out his plan.

But now as he raced along hoping to get near enough to "Patch" for the well-trained horse to hear his voice, Ted was ready to cry with anger and disappointment; he realized that his attempt to run away from home and join the Northern Army was already defeated, for Mr. Webb had promptly refused, months earlier, to give Ted permission for such an undertaking.

Kathleen had awakened later than any of the other adventurous early risers, although she happily believed herself to be the first one awake, excepting Hitty, of course; who, Kathleen was convinced, must always be up before sunrise; and when the little girl now appeared in the kitchen Hitty raised both hands in wonder as she exclaimed:

"Whateber get yo' up dis hour?" and Kathleen smilingly explained about the May baskets, and her plan to hang them on the door of the twins' chamber; "and I'll read you the verses I've written," she added, and Hitty listened with occasional exclamations of admiring praise as the little girl read the May day verses.

"Dose are gran' pomes, Miss Kathie!" she declared solemnly, "an' now yo' jes' make way wid dis porridge 'fo' yo' start forth," and Kathleen was quite ready to eat the bowl of hot oatmeal porridge and cream that Hitty offered her.

This kitchen visit, however, had taken time, so that when Kathleen was ready to start for the ledge the sun was well up and Kathleen knew she had no time to lose or the twins would be coming downstairs before she could return.

She found her baskets among the ferns, the violets still fresh in the damp moss, and fastening the papers on which the verses were written to the baskets she turned back to the house and found her father and mother standing in the kitchen doorway.

"I'm going to hang these baskets on the door of the twins' room," Kathleen explained, holding up the flower-filled baskets, sure that her father and mother would admire them.

"But where are the twins?" asked Mrs. Webb; "their chamber door is wide open and they are not in their room. I supposed they were with you."

CHAPTER VI

ADELAIDE MARY

When it was discovered that Ted, "Patch" and "Frisk," as well as Janet and Beth, had disappeared, Mr. and Mrs. Webb decided that it was some sort of a May morning celebration planned by Ted as a surprise for the little Ross girls.

"Ted has evidently taken them for a morning ride, and they will all have a fine appetite for breakfast. I think, Hitty, it will be a good plan to make an extra pan of popovers," said Mrs. Webb, as she and Kathleen, May baskets in hand, went toward the front of the house.

"I think Ted might have taken me, too," said Kathleen, starting up the stairs with her flower-filled baskets; "'Frisk' is *my* pony, and I think Ted hadn't any business to take him off this way. And Janet and Beth are *my* company!" declared Kathleen, disappointed over the fact that apparently she had been completely left out of this early celebration of May day. For thee moment Kathleen forgot all her plans to do everything possible for the Ross twins, and she was angry at Ted, and did not even hear her mother's response as she ran toward her own chamber.

For a moment Kathleen was resolved to destroy the pretty baskets, and to tear up the carefully written verses; there were tears in her blue eyes as she turned toward the corner of her room and whispered: "Well, Adelaide Mary, I like you better than any girl there is, even if I am eleven years old and you only a doll," and from a small wooden rocking-chair Kathleen lifted a huge doll. Adelaide Mary had journeyed all the way from Maine in Kathleen's arms; but that was four years ago, and for the past year Kathleen had not so constantly desired the company of the cherished doll, whose big china head with black painted ringlets, red cheeks and blue eyes, had so long seemed beautiful to the little girl.

Adelaide Mary was dressed in a gown of green plaided silk, with white kid slippers, and she wore a tiny round hat wreathed with little flowers; Kathleen had made everything that Adelaide Mary wore, and as she lifted the doll, in spite of feeling hurt and angry at what she believed was Ted's slight, a little smile crept over her face and she whispered: "*You* never do hateful things, Adelaide Mary; you're always just the same," and holding the doll in her arms Kathleen went toward the window and stood looking out, feeling a little comforted by Adelaide Mary's silent, faithful presence.

The usual hour for breakfast came and Mrs. Webb called Kathleen, saying: "Ted and the girls will have to take whatever Hitty pleases to give them," and Kathleen, still holding Adelaide Mary, followed Aunt Mel into the dining-room. Mrs. Webb smiled as her little daughter drew up a chair beside her own and carefully seated the doll.

"Why, this seems like old times, when Adelaide Mary was always with us," she said. "Since you began making rugs, Kathleen, you haven't had much time for Adelaide, have you?"

Kathleen shook her head soberly; she was thinking to herself that May day was spoiled, that Ted and Janet and Beth had taken her very own pony and were probably having a fine time galloping about the fields, and none of them had wanted her. The choky feeling, that Kathleen so dreaded, prevented her from speaking aloud as she remembered this. And when Aunty Mel said: "I don't see whatever possessed Ted to take the twins off at so early an hour," Kathleen gave her a look of loving approval. Aunty Mel, she thought, was even a better friend than poor silent Adelaide Mary, and when

breakfast was over the little girl kept very close to
Miss Mel as they all went out in the yard to see if
there was any sign of Ted and his companions'
return. But it was a full hour after breakfast when
Kathleen, with Adelaide Mary in her arms, standing near the lilac bushes, saw a queer little caval-
cade coming along the road. "Patch" led the way,
with Janet and Beth on his back; beside him walked
Ted, leading the brown pony, and Kathleen's glance
was quick to discover that "Frisk" limped, and at
this she wholly forgot Adelaide Mary and the doll
slipped from her grasp to the branches of a stout little privet bush where it lay staring up at its careless
owner. But Kathleen was off like a flash, and as the
tired and disappointed Ted, who was limping a little
himself, turned into the driveway Kathleen was
there to meet him calling out:

"What have you done to my pony, you hateful Ted
Webb?"

But before Ted could respond Beth came scrambling down from the back of the patient "Patch," her
round face tear-stained and bruised from a recent
tumble, her dark curls tangled and untidy, and her
voice broken and unhappy as she stammered out:
"It's my fault, Kathleen. Truly it is; I let 'Frisk' out
of the stable——"

Then to Kathleen's amazement Janet was beside Beth declaring, between sobs, that she was to blame. "I stole Ted's horse and then it ran away, and I fell off and hurt my wrist," she said to the accusing and startled Kathleen.

By this time Miss Mel had reached the little group, and she examined Janet's bruised hand and wrist a little anxiously, and led her toward the house followed by Beth and Kathleen. Mr. Webb and Ted went to the stable, and Ted told his father the whole story of the morning's adventure: of Janet being thrown from the back of "Patch," of the discovery of Beth resting beside the road, and of finding the discouraged pony grazing in a near-by field. "Those girls might have been killed," Ted had declared, as he told his father that Janet and Beth had each planned to "practice" riding horseback.

As Ted talked Mr. Webb had unstrapped his knapsack from the saddle, and now turned a questioning look toward his son, and Ted nodded as if in answer. "Yes, Father! I was off to join the army. I knew it was no use to ask you again, and you know the any needs men, President Lincoln has asked for men," and the fifteen-year-old boy straightened his shoulders, his face serious and anxious as if he were responsible for the success or failure of the Northern cause.

"Yes, Ted, I know," Mr. Webb responded soberly; and in the talk that followed there was no word of blame for Ted; nevertheless as they turned toward the house the boy had finally resolved that he would never again run away from home, and that when he joined the army, as he still meant to do, his father and mother should know of his intention.

"After all, Ted, it proves fortunate that 'Patch' was saddled when little Miss Janet decided to ride horseback," said Mr. Webb, and Ted responded quickly:

"And that I was in time to find the girls, and 'Patch' and 'Frisk,' before more damage was done."

Ted ate a hearty breakfast, his mother keeping his plate well filled with crisp bacon and scrambled eggs as she, too, listened to his story of the morning's adventures.

Hitty carried a tray up to the front chamber where Janet, with her left hand neatly bandaged by Miss Mel, sat in a low cushioned chair on one side of a small round table facing Beth, whose bruised cheek had been tenderly cared for. Both the little girls were wearing dresses of Kathleen's, as their own had been soiled and torn so badly that Miss Mel knew they could not again be worn.

Hitty set the tray on the little round table. "I'se gwine ter fetch up hot batter cakes an' honey in jes'

a minute," she announced, and trotted off, and
Kathleen helped Janet and Beth to hot porridge,
filled the pretty blue mugs with hot cocoa, and said
happily: "It's fun to have breakfast up-stairs," and
Janet and Beth both nodded solemnly. They had
hardly spoken since declaring their blame in regard
to "Patch" and "Frisk"; and they were both
ashamed and sorry for the trouble they had so evidently caused by their thoughtlessness. Janet and
Beth were sure that Kathleen must be angry toward
them, and they were both a little homesick and had
quite forgotten the beautiful muslin dresses, and
even that it was May day; and when, as they began
eating the porridge, Kathleen without a word suddenly darted from the room, Janet leaned across the
table and whispered:

"She's mad at us. She's run away!" and tears gathered in Beth's hazel eyes as she nodded her agree-
ment and stammered: "O-oh, Janet, I—I wish we
were home."

But before either of them could say anything more
Kathleen was back again, a flower-filled basket in
each hand, and smiling so radiantly that Janet and
Beth found themselves smiling in response; and
when they discovered that the baskets had been
made especially for them, and read the May day vers-

es, their troubles were forgotten and they were again the happy little girls who had arrived at the farm.

"It's too late for our picnic, Aunty Mel says," said Kathleen, as Hitty appeared with hot cakes and honey, "and I guess you are both too tired, anyway?"

Janet and Beth owned they were tired; and now Beth became a little mournful again as she remembered they had spoiled the well-worn frocks that their mother had so carefully mended for them to wear on, this visit, and Kathleen was quick to notice Beth's sober face, and said quickly:

"Your mother will have to put tucks in those dresses, even if I have outgrown them. You see, being a year older makes a lot of difference," she explained; and as the twins realized that the pretty dresses they were wearing were now their very own Janet exclaimed:

"Whatever makes you give us so many things?" and her glance was so affectionate and kind that Kathleen smiled delightedly, realizing that it was a lot more fun to make presents than she had ever before realized, and as Ted called her from the open door, and nodded approvingly as he noticed the girls' smiling faces, Kathleen suddenly remembered Adelaide Mary, and jumped up exclaiming:

"Oh, whatever has become of her!"

"If you mean Adelaide Mary, why I can tell you! I found her in the garden and she's downstairs," said Ted, going on toward his own room. "I'll run down and get her," said Kathleen, and darted off.

"Who is 'Adelaide Mary' ?" asked Beth in a whisper, and Janet shook her head as she responded: "Oh! I s'pose it's some other girl come to visit Kathleen," and the twins became very silent, for they were both a little disappointed to think of a strange girl coming to share their visit.

In a moment they heard Kathleen's voice saying: "Yes, Adelaide Mary, I forgot all about you, poor dear, but I love you just the same," and the twins again had a twinge of homesickness, thinking that this Adelaide Mary, of whom they had never before heard, must surely be Kathleen's dearest friend; but almost before they had reached this decision Kathleen was in the room, and in her arms was a big doll wearing a dress of plaided green silk, and Kathleen was saying:

"Here is Adelaide Mary!"

CHAPTER VII

SELLING A RUG

IT was late in the afternoon when Miss Melvina and the little Ross girls started for their drive home. Kathleen stood at the gate, with Adelaide Mary in her arms, and looked after them soberly, for she was greatly disappointed when her mother had refused permission for her little daughter to return home with her aunt; and Kathleen now told herself that the box with the two gold pieces would never be found. "I might just as well not look for it after so long a time," she decided, and resolved to at once consult Hitty as to possible purchasers of hooked rugs, and for the time Kathleen endeavored to comfort herself by the remembrance of the twins' delight in their white muslin dresses, and that they had started for home happy in the possession of much better frocks than they had worn on their arrival at the Webb farm; and although she repeated to herself the fact that these dresses were worth as much as the lost money, Kathleen found but little satisfaction in that fact, and as the days passed she became more and more determined to earn enough to give the twins the money she had lost; and Mrs. Webb was not a little puzzled to find that Kathleen through the pleasant spring weather seemed to like nothing as well as to sit at the rug frame drawing the bits of green wool through the loosely woven burlap; and Hitty was sadly puzzled by the little girl's constant appeals for advice as to the way to sell a rug; and the good-natured colored girl decided that her young mistress wanted to sell the rug in order to secure money for a present for some member of the family, and did her best to be of use, and she encouraged Kathleen to believe it would be an easy matter to find a customer who would gladly pay five dollars for a "pine-tree" rug.

It was now the end of May, 1863; the Union forces under General Hooker had suffered defeat at Chancellorsville, with a loss of killed and wounded of thirty thousand men; and now more than ever did the Confederates feel that they could not be conquered, and General Lee confidently expected that he could invade Northern territory, perhaps even conquer a peace on the soil of the loyal states. Ted and his father and mother realized that every day brought such a danger near; and even Kathleen, absorbed as she was in her determination to restore the missing gold pieces and tell Aunty Mel, as well as Janet and Beth, the story of the "joke," did not declare, as she had formerly, that she hoped the splendid Lee would come to Gettysburg that she might see him. For gradually the little girl was coming to realize that an invading army, no matter how great and splendid its commanding general may be, is something to be feared, and even as she questioned Hitty Kathleen recalled what her father had said to Ted that very morning. "You may be a soldier within a month, my boy; for if Lee's troops come this way we will all have to fight," Mr. Webb had said, and Kathleen remembered Ted's sober face as he responded: "I'd do my best, sir;" and now the little girl, without waiting for Hitty's answer as to a possible purchaser of the rug, suddenly exclaimed: "Oh, Hitty! Whatever will we do if war comes to Gettysburg?"

"My lan', I reckons we wouldn't do nuthin', missy! But w'ot yo' a-trubblin' 'bout de war fer? I'm a-projectin' a way fer yo' ter sell dat rug, an' I'se puzzled it out. Yas'm! I knows how it can be sold!" and Hitty's face beamed with satisfaction, as Kathleen eagerly demanded to hear Hitty's plan.

"Dis am de way, shu' as yo're born, Missy Kathleen. Now yo' lis'en! Fust of all yo' kin say to yo' ma dat yo' tinks yo'll jes' ride yo' pony down de road, maybe as fur as Mrs. McPherson's; dat'll be all right," and Hitty nodded reassuringly. "An' yo' kin, take along yo' rug, an' yo' kin show it ter Mrs. McPherson, an' sorter point out ter her how fine 'tis, an' she'll prob'ly 'clar to goodness dat she wan's ter buy it!" and the triumphant Hitty drew a long breath of satisfaction as if Kathleen's rug had surely found a purchaser.

"Oh, Hitty! I do believe that is a good plan. I'll go to-morrow," declared Kathleen, "and perhaps Mrs. McPherson may know of someone who will buy the other one."

"Wot 'odder one' ?" asked the amazed Hitty.

"Why, the other one I am going to make! You see, Hitty, I must earn ten dollars, two five dollar gold pieces," Kathleen explained.

"Wal, den w'y don' yo' jes' ask ten dollars fer *dis* rug?" questioned Hitty hopefully, but Kathleen shook her head. It seemed to her a little doubtful that anyone would pay even five dollars; and she resolved that if she were offered even two dollars for the rug she must take it: "then I'll have to make five rugs," she thought, "and that would take all summer." Nevertheless Kathleen was very hopeful that her pretty "pine-tree" rug would find a customer in Mrs. McPherson. "And if she doesn't want it I know just what I'll do. I'll ride on and stop at each house until somebody does buy it," she resolved; and the next morning she asked her mother if she might not ride "Frisk" over to the McPherson farm, several miles distant.

"'Frisk' isn't lame now, and Ted says I ought to ride him every day," she explained, and Mrs. Webb had agreed that if the next day was pleasant Kathleen might ride over to see Mrs. McPherson.

"And you had best wear your new pink gingham," said Mrs. Webb.

"And my new hat?" questioned Kathleen hopefully, for her new hat of white straw, with a big pink rose just under the left brim, seemed to the little girl exactly the right hat to wear on such an errand as hers, and her mother's smiling reply that "All new hats have to be worn the first time, don't they!" sent Kathleen racing upstairs to draw the hat from its bandbox and lay it on the table so that she would not fail to see it when she awoke the next morning; and as she held the pretty hat up to admire its fresh beauty Kathleen told herself that her mother was surely the loveliest mother a little girl could have. "She's always pleasant," Kathleen thought gratefully.

The next morning, the last day of May, proved clear and pleasant; and Hitty had carried the rug, carefully wrapped, to the stable add fastened the clumsy bundle to the front of Kathleen's saddle, and it was

Hitty who earnestly insisted on seeing the little girl safely started on her ride, and directly after breakfast Kathleen bade her mother good-bye and, followed by Hitty, ran into the yard where "Frisk," all saddled and ready to start, awaited her.

"Now, Missy Kathie, don't yo' fergit ter smile w'en yo' offers dat rug!" Hitty solemnly warned her as Kathleen, wearing the new plaided pink gingham and the pretty hat, gathered up the reins and prepared to start, and Kathleen nodded and with a word to "Frisk" rode down the driveway and turned the pony's head down the road leading toward South Mountain, rising proudly in the distance. "Frisk" trotted along nearly as happy as his young mistress to be out on the smooth road in the fragrant air. Kathleen's copper colored hair flew back from her face and her blue eyes were bright with pleasure as she thought hopefully that perhaps before the end of another month she could give Aunty Mel a white box containing two five dollar gold pieces; but beneath her happy thoughts was the wish that she had promptly confessed to her aunt the moment she knew of the loss. That would have been so much easier.

That very morning Mrs. Webb had asked Kathleen what she meant to do with the rug, and Kathleen had impulsively responded: "I am going to sell it and give the money to the Ross girls," and Mrs. Webb had replied that would be a very good plan, but beyond her approving thought that Kathleen was surely the most generous-hearted girl in the world, she gave it no further consideration, but Kathleen now remembered it, and smiled to herself as she thought of her mother's surprise when she should come trotting home from her ride with the price of the rug in her pocket.

"Frisk" was now climbing a steep hill and at the top he came to a standstill, looking over his shoulder as if to tell his rider it was time for a fat pony to rest; and Kathleen quite understood him, and laughed delightedly as she dismounted and led him into the shade of a wide-spreading oak. From where she stood Kathleen could look over broad fields and slopes of cultivated farmlands toward the heights of ridges and mountains; there were deep forests, and sheltering groves, and gently flowing streams, and turning toward the highway she could see the town of Gettysburg, nestled among fields and hills and sparkling in the May sunshine, with Oak Ridge rising beyond it: Oak Ridge, on which stood the seminary, and where Kathleen was sure the missing box had been lost; and as the little girl's glance traveled over valley and forest she told herself that it would be an easy matter to ride "Frisk" straight to Oak Ridge; either of the broad highways would lead to it.

"I'll go! It's only four miles!" she exclaimed. "I'll have plenty of time to ride 'Frisk' over and get home in good season; and maybe I can find the box. Oh! if I only could find it!" and in another moment she had mounted the surprised and somewhat disapproving pony and was urging him over the road toward Oak Ridge at his best pace.

CHAPTER VIII

THE WRONG ROAD

OAK RIDGE, that only a few weeks later was to be renamed and henceforth known as "Seminary" Ridge by the contending armies, is crossed by a number of roads, and Kathleen was sure she could find her way without entering the town of Gettysburg or running any chance of being seen by her Aunt Mel or any acquaintances.

"But if I do find the box I'll take it straight to Aunty Mel; and if I don't find the box I'll sell this rug. I'll begin just as Hitty told me to by asking Mrs. McPherson if she would like to see a pretty hooked rug that I have just made," and Kathleen smiled happily thinking that this pleasant springtime road was sure to lead her to the end of all her worries about the lost box.

Now and then her glance rested on the carefully rolled rug, and she had a fleeting wish that she had brought Adelaide Mary for company; for Kathleen had had so few playmates that her doll really meant a sense of companionship for her.

"But I guess carrying a doll wouldn't look very grown-up," she decided; and in selling a rug a doll would perhaps look too childish, and her thoughts flew to the remembrance of her father's talk that morning at the breakfast table; he had said that no one could say at what place the Confederates would enter Pennsylvania, and that there were rumors of Southern soldiers already on the march, and he had added that probably their scouts were everywhere on the alert, and he had referred to the two whose conversation at the ledge Kathleen had overheard some weeks before.

Kathleen wondered, as the pony trotted briskly over the smooth road, if, as the Union soldier had said, her remembrance of that conversation had proved a help to the Northern Army, a warning of a possible invasion of Northern states; and the little girl recalled Ted's serious determination to become a soldier, and wished there was some way in which a little Yankee girl could, if war really came near her home, be of use.

"But I do wish General Robert E. Lee was on our side," she thought; although she could not know that Lee's loyalty to his own state and what it stood for was one of the reasons why all men, and even a little Yankee girl from far-away Maine, admired him.

Kathleen had been so intent on her thoughts, so well pleased with the pony's even pace and the soft warm air, that she had not given much attention to the direction. Now looking about her there was no familiar object in sight; but the little girl felt no uneasiness. She felt sure the road would soon bring her in sight of Oak Ridge, and she did not know that "Frisk" had turned at a curve of the highway into a road leading toward Harrisburg and was going directly away from the seminary. For the pony's former home lay in than direction, and the little creature had not been away from it long enough to forget the roads that would lead him back.

Now and then some farmer would drive past Kathleen waving her a friendly greeting, and when an old wagon, pulled by a tired grey horse and driven by a man in worn, shabby clothes stopped directly in front of the pony so that "Frisk" was also obliged to stop, Kathleen was not at all frightened and smiled a greeting at the driver who had not, she supposed, seen the pony in time to turn out for her; but the driver of the dilapidated wagon did not move or speak and Kathleen gazed at him in sudden alarm.

"I do believe he's asleep!" she exclaimed, and at the moment the man's eyes opened and he stared as if as deeply surprised as Kathleen herself.

"What road is this?" he questioned sharply, straightening his shoulders briskly.

"I'm afraid I don't know; only it goes near the seminary on Oak Ridge," Kathleen responded, and at this the man's face became alert and he jumped from his old wagon so quickly that the little girl stared at him wonderingly.

"Surely not! What a fool I am to get off my course like that," he muttered, and backing the tired horse he turned it in the same direction in which the pony was headed, and then gave another sharp look at the little girl in her pretty dress and hat riding the fat brown pony.

"Are you bound for the seminary, young lady?" he asked, and Kathleen smilingly replied: "Yes, sir," and would have started the pony on past the wagon but the man's hand rested on "Frisk's" bridle-rein.

"Not so fast. You surely want to help a traveler who has lost his way," he said, after Kathleen again replied:

"Yes, sir! But I thought it likely you were a farmer, and perhaps knew the way better than I do. And I surely do not see Oak Ridge," and the little girl sent a puzzled look along the broad highway in the direction where she supposed the seminary to be.

"I'll wager you don't know any better than I do," muttered the man, "even if you were born in Gettysburg."

"Oh! I wasn't born in Gettysburg. I was born in Maine," Kathleen promptly announced, and now the man's dark eyes rested on her with even a sharper interest as he said:

"A little Yankee girl, eh? And I suppose your father is a Yankee soldier," and without waiting for an answer he asked sharply: "What are you going to the seminary for?"

"I lost a box there. I lost it a month ago; a little white box with two gold pieces in it!" Kathleen said soberly; and, at the man's exclamation, she continued: "And nobody knows it!"

"Then no one knows that you are bound there this morning?" said the man thoughtfully.

"No, sir; I started out to sell my 'pine-tree' rug; it's in this bundle," and Kathleen touched the roll fastened to the front of her saddle. She did not feel at all afraid of this dark-eyed stranger whose pleasant voice had so friendly a sound; and she went on to tell him that "Frisk" had been a present on her eleventh birthday; and when he smiled and said that he hoped when his own little daughter was eleven that she might have a pony exactly like "Frisk," Kathleen began to feel that she had made a friend.

"Where is your little girl?" she asked, thinking how pleasant it would be if this strange little girl could come and visit her and learn to ride "Frisk," but the man only shook his head saying: "Far away, little Yankee girl," in so sad a voice that for the first time Kathleen began to wonder about him, and now ventured to ask:

"What is your little girl's name?

But at that moment "Frisk" swerved from the highway into a narrow road going so rapidly that Kathleen had to do her best to control him, but she could hear the rattle of the wagon coming behind her and realized the stranger was following. The road grew suddenly narrow and Kathleen found herself gazing over "Frisk's" head at a solidly built fence before which the pony stopped apparently as surprised as Kathleen; and a moment later the stranger was standing beside "Frisk," his glance fixed angrily on Kathleen.

"What sort of a trap is this you've led me into? Telling me you were on the right road to the seminary and I, fool enough to believe a Yankee, turning back on my course. We've been riding straight away from Gettysburg!" he declared, and drawing a worn silver watch from his pocket he held it up. "Look at the time! Twelve o'clock!"

"Oh, my goodness!" exclaimed the astonished Kathleen. "And 'twas not nine when I left home. I must indeed have taken the wrong road; and poor 'Frisk' must be tired," and without a glance at the stranger Kathleen slid from her saddle and began smoothing the pony's head and promising him he should have a drink and something to eat, and as the Confederate scout listened he gave a quick breath of relief and his face softened, for he knew that this little girl had not purposely misled him, but had, as she said, lost her own way.

"I can hear the noise of a brook, and my poor horse will welcome a drink. I'll unhitch him and lead them both down to the creek," said the man in his former kindly tone, and in a few moments he was leading the two tired animals through the little grove toward Rock Creek, while Kathleen leaned against the stout fence and wondered to what part of the world the brown pony had brought her.

"I must start home as soon as 'Frisk' is rested," she thought a little anxiously, knowing that even now her mother and Hitty would be expecting her return, but her thoughts were interrupted by the sound of the breaking of branches and "Frisk" dashed through the underbrush as if pursued by some dangerous foe and came to a standstill with his nose against the gate close beside his small mistress.

"Why, 'Frisk'! whatever is the matter!" asked the startled girl, looking about for some sign of danger.

But the woods and fields seemed deserted; there was no sound to be heard save the squawk of a distant blue jay and scolding chitter of a curious grey squirrel that had come along the top of the fence not far from the gate.

Kathleen, with her hand on the pony's bridle-rein, stood looking anxiously toward the creek. Every moment she expected to hear steps and to see the shabby stranger and his grey horse appear from among the trees; but time passed, and, beyond "Frisk's" uneasy movements, nothing disturbed the quiet.

Kathleen was sure that her pony had not had his much needed drink, and she was now thirsty herself, as well as hungry, and, deciding that the stranger had perhaps rode off leaving his wagon to its fate, she resolved to lead "Frisk" back and search for a place where they could both drink. "And then we'll start back the way we came," she thought.

But before venturing into the underbrush Kathleen took off her pretty hat and put it carefully on the seat of the old wagon. "I guess it will be safe there," she thought, and leading the willing "Frisk" she turned toward the slope that led, she was quite sure, to a stream; and the little girl quickly realized that she had been wise to leave her hat on the wagon-seat, for brambles and thorny branches caught at her dress and she had to watch carefully that she did not slip, until at last pushing through a thick growth of bushes, with the pony resolutely pulling back, Kathleen exclaimed aloud, for she found herself almost at the edge of a steep rocky bank below which flowed the creek, and over which, had not "Frisk" so steadily held back, she might easily have plunged. She had a glimpse of Oak Ridge in the distance, but had no time to look, for "Frisk," now eager to reach the stream, was pulling strongly toward a rocky slope at the left, and he now became guide and leader as Kathleen, clinging to his mane, stumbled on beside him until they reached the edge of the stream where she succeeded in slipping the bits from the pony's mouth so that he might drink in comfort; and then with a broad oak leaf Kathleen made a clumsy cup from which she could drink.

It proved a little difficult to persuade "Frisk" to come out of the water into which he had eagerly waded, but after a little he made his slow way toward a grassy point that stretched into the stream, and was about to settle down on his side to roll over when Kathleen's sharp call prevented.

"I guess I'd better take off your saddle," Kathleen said, reluctant to delay her start for home, yet sure that her pony would rest more quickly if free from his burden; so she unstrapped the saddle and carried it a short distance up the bank, and then put the rug beside it; she felt sure the pony was too tired to go any further for the present, and that he would feed on the young grass near by.

"I'm tired myself," thought Kathleen, "and I do wish I'd thought to take a luncheon," and she had just seated herself with her back against the saddle when she heard a voice, that seemed to come from the foot of the rocky slope:

"Hullo! Little Yankee girl! Little Yankee girl!" it called.

CHAPTER IX

OVER THE CLIFF

KATHLEEN jumped up with an exclamation of surprise and instantly called back: "I'm right here on the slope!" and stood waiting; for, although she looked eagerly in the direction from which the voice came, there was no one to be seen.

"I'm hurt! Fell over the cliff," came the response, and in an instant Kathleen was running toward the foot of that wooded cliff over which she herself had so nearly tumbled.

Just as she reached the bottom a number of good-sized rocks came crashing through the bushes and rolled down very near where she was standing, and the man called again:

"I don't know as you can climb up here, and I don't know as you can help me. I reckon my ankle is broken; and beside that I'm wedged between rocks."

"I'm sure I can help you," Kathleen called eagerly. "I know I can climb up there. Anyway, I'm sure there's a farmhouse up beyond that house and I can run up there and get someone."

"No! no!" called the man. "Promise not to bring anyone here. Promise!" he repeated, his voice shrill and anxious, so that the puzzled little girl instantly called back:

"I will do whatever you tell me!"

"That's right. Then try and come up toward the right of the scrub oak, and then you'll see me," he replied, "and maybe I can throw you down a package that I'll want you to carry to Gettysburg for me. But you must come carefully," he cautioned, and Kathleen began to make her way among the rough underbrush and rocks at the base of the cliff, looking up at long stretches of smooth rock that made her realize how great a danger she had escaped when "Frisk" had so sturdily pulled her back.

"I guess it's lucky the man got wedged in the rock after all," she thought, as she scrambled up the face of a ledge where occasional stout little spruce trees had rooted themselves in crevices and gave her something to hold fast to.

As she reached the top of this ledge the man called again:

"Well done, little Yankee girl! Look up now and you'll see me." And looking up Kathleen exclaimed in surprise, and with a little note of alarm in her voice, as she saw the dark face of the stranger peering over a high rock that seemed about to pitch over the face of the cliff.

But as Kathleen stood gazing up at her new acquaintance she noticed there were crevices along the ledge, and small spruce trees here and there, and she felt sure she could reach the point where the man was imprisoned.

"I'm coming up. It's good climbing," she told him hopefully, and again the man cautioned her anxiously to be careful, and the little girl resolutely began to make her way upwards. Now and then her foot slipped and but for her clutch on some pliant little sapling she must have fallen. Once or twice a loose rock gave way beneath her feet and only her quickness then saved her. Although it seemed a long time it was but a few moments before Kathleen found herself at the edge of the narrow crevice in which the man had fallen. He was standing, his back against a wall of stone, the rising ledge directly in front of him to the height of his shoulders, and his face was bruised and scratched.

As Kathleen appeared he drew a long breath of evident relief and smiled with so much approval that Kathleen smiled in response, and said: "Now I'll help you get down!"

"I begin to believe you will," declared the man, "but I don't know just how. Look!" and he nodded toward the left, and Kathleen, stepping into the crevice, could see that his feet were both wedged firmly beneath a mass of rock.

"That rock came down with me!" said the man, "and it would take a good while to dig it off my feet; and I reckon my feet, from the way they feel, are pretty well smashed. I wish to goodness you and your fat pony had been in Egypt before I ever met up with you," and a scowl crept over his dark face as the man remembered that but for this girl he would by this time be in possession of the information he wanted in regard to the supplies of food and the number of horses that Confederates could secure near Gettysburg; for this shabby traveler was one of the many scouts sent out in advance of Lee's army, that was already moving north, and the scout knew that this delay on his part might prove a serious matter. He had scribbled a letter to his commanding officer giving directions as to the supplies obtainable near Harrisburg, the capital of Pennsylvania, and which Lee had resolved to capture, and the man decided when he called Kathleen to his aid that this little Yankee girl should be his messenger if it proved, as he now felt sure it must, that he could not go on himself.

Kathleen's face flushed; she wanted to tell the man that he need not have followed the pony; but she was now eager to help him and said again: "I'm sure I can pull those rocks off."

"No! I tried it. They go crashing and rolling down the cliff making enough noise to rouse a city!" declared the man, and added quickly, "I don't want anyone to think me fool enough to tumble over a cliff."

But Kathleen was already tugging and pulling at one of the big rocks between which the man's feet were so firmly wedged; and, in spite of his evident fear of the noise, he leaned forward and endeavored to help her. Once or twice she succeeded in raising it a little but not enough for the man to free himself, and as the heavy stone settled back he groaned with pain, and Kathleen looked up at him anxiously and said: "If I slip another rock under the next time we start it maybe that will help." He did not reply, except by a nod, and Kathleen began to fear that he was seriously hurt, and turned back to tug at the rock with a new determination to set him free, and as the rock moved she succeeded in kicking a smaller stone under it so this time it could not fall back, and by a great effort the imprisoned man and the little girl succeeded in moving it sufficiently for him to free his feet. As he did so he sank back with a moan of pain and Kathleen realized that he could not stand, that his feet were badly hurt, and for a moment the little girl hardly knew what to do unless she broke her promise and hurried off to bring help. But the man drew himself into a sitting posture and began to draw off his heavy clumsy shoes. These had, in a measure, protected his feet, but he was evidently in pain.

"I'd give a good deal for a bucket of cold water," he said as if speaking to himself, and Kathleen remembered the tin bucket that hung from the back of his rickety wagon.

"I'll bring it!" she declared. "I can climb up from here and get the bucket and bring some water."

"You're a good soldier!" said the man, his glance resting kindly on the little girl who seemed now to think only of helping this unknown stranger. "I reckon I'll have to let you try," he added thoughtfully, as if he was sorry to make trouble for her.

"There's a box of food in that wagon," he continued. "I reckon we could both do with a bite? And there's a blanket," and although he did not suggest that Kathleen should attempt to bring these things the little girl instantly resolved that she would make as many trips to the wagon as was needful to secure them, and now started off to discover an easy path up the cliff.

Turning to the right she followed the ledge until it gradually grew less steep, and although the way was rough she climbed steadily on, and just before reaching the wooded top she heard a bubbling sound and looked about anxiously. "That sounds like a brook," she thought; but it was not a brook; it was a spring of clear water that came bubbling up at the foot of a ledge just above where Kathleen was standing.

"It looks just like our spring!" she exclaimed, and for a moment a sense of fear and homesickness tempted the little girl to forget her promise to the injured stranger, and to find some farmhouse where help would be sent to him and then go straight to her home.

But it was only for a moment; for Kathleen remembered the man's words, "You're a good soldier," and the thought, too, of the stranger's own little girl, who was far away, made her resolve not to desert him but to do her best to help him; and after a drink of the cool water she hurried over the short distance to the deserted road and the old wagon.

After unfastening the bucket, Kathleen drew a pasteboard box from under the wagon-seat, and a rolled up blanket. The box would go in the bucket, and she was sure she could carry both blanket and pail down to the crevice in the cliff.

And now the little girl turned to look at her pretty hat resting on the worn leather cushion of the wagon-seat. "I guess I'll put it under the seat," she decided, and pulling a handful of tall brakes she spread them on the dusty bottom of the old wagon and put her hat on them under the shelter of the seat; then taking up bucket and blanket she started back.

At the spring she left the blanket and the box of food. "I guess I can manage to carry the pail half-full," she thought; and, in spite of the rough way, Kathleen succeeded in reaching the crevice with the pail half-filled with spring water.

The man drank thirstily, and then began to bathe his swollen feet and ankles with the cool water.

"If I only had something to bandage them with," he muttered.

"Would the flounce on my dress do?" asked Kathleen, looking regretfully at her new pink gingham dress, the pink dress that only that morning had been so fresh and pretty and that now was soiled and torn by her scrambles among rocks and briers.

"Indeed it would. I'll cut the stitches with my knife, and you shall never be sorry for it," declared the man earnestly, as he drew out a clasp knife, and with careful hands ripped off the wide flounce. Kathleen's ready fingers helped him fasten the wet bandages about his ankles, and when this was done she sped back to the spring and brought the food and blanket.

"It's too warm to want a blanket, but maybe 'twill be good for your feet," she said, as almost too tired to take another step the little girl sank down on a moss-covered rock at the entrance of the crevice.

The man made no response but opened the box and held it out to Kathleen.

"Thank you. I am dreadful hungry," she said, so soberly that the man smiled, and bade her help herself, and Kathleen took a square of hard gingerbread from the box, a slice of chicken and a biscuit, and handed the box back to her companion, who now asked if she had seen anything of the grey horse.

Kathleen shook her head; she had entirely forgotten about the grey horse, and the man said it had probably made its way into some near-by field.

"I'd find Old Ned quickly enough if I could walk," he said.

"My pony is down by the creek," said Kathleen, and her companion nodded thoughtfully.

"You must rest an hour, and then lead your pony back to the road and start back to Gettysburg. I want you to take a letter for me," he continued, "and you must tell me your name and where your home is."

"But how will you get along without me?" asked Kathleen, but her face brightened as she realized that very soon she would be on "Frisk's" back bound toward home.

"I'll manage. I'll crawl to the spring. Then I'll be all right," he declared; and an hour later, with Kathleen tugging the bucket and blanket, he did indeed crawl within reach of the bubbling water, where he sank down exhausted.

"Now, little Yankee girl, here is a letter that must reach Gettysburg post-office to-night."

Kathleen took the white envelope that the man drew from his pocket, and said soberly, "I'll try and not lose it."

"You *mustn't* lose it," he warned her. "You have a pocket, haven't you?"

Kathleen nodded. "Yes, a deep pocket!" she replied, and the man smiled as he handed her the letter which she put carefully in her pocket.

"Now here is something you are not to look at until you get home," he said, giving Kathleen a small firm package. "It's a present," he added, noticing her wondering look.

"Thank you. I won't look at it until I get home," said Kathleen, smiling as she thought of her mother's surprise when she should hear of the day's adventure.

"Now be off. You brought me into this trouble, but you have proved yourself a friend and a soldier," said the man, and his thin brown fingers clasped Kathleen's hand as he bade her good-bye.

"Please give my love to your little girl," Kathleen called over her shoulder as she started toward the creek.

"Indeed I will, little Yankee girl," the man responded, adding to himself: "If I ever see my little girl again," for he well knew the dangers before him, not only in his work as a scout for the Confederate Army, but the dangers of the great battle between the Northern and Southern armies that was day by day drawing near.

"HERE IS A LETTER THAT MUST REACH THE GETTYSBURG
POST-OFFICE TONIGHT"

CHAPTER X

"BUTTONS"

"Frisk" was easily caught, and Kathleen led him as near as possible to the place where she had left her saddle and the rug; and as she looked at the rug the little girl suddenly resolved to climb up to the spring and give the rug to the man who, she felt sure, must remain there for the coming night.

"It will be something like a bed, anyway," decided Kathleen, for the moment forgetting her debt to the little Ross girls as well as her plan to sell the rug, and thinking only of the look of pain on the stranger's face; and remembering that, after all, it was indeed "Frisk's" dash from the highway that had led the traveler to his tumble over the cliff.

"And he gave me a present," she replied. "Maybe it's soldiers' buttons!" and at this thought a little smile crept over her face; for in 1863, every little Yankee girl was eager to possess a number of the shining brass buttons with the raised, winged eagle, that were used on the soldiers' coats.

Fastening "Frisk's" bridle-rein to a stout sapling Kathleen picked up the closely rolled rug and started back up the slope to the spring. This was a much easier climb than the one she had made up to the rocky crevice, and she was soon within hearing of the bubbling waters of the spring, and called: "I'm bringing you something," and rounded the ledge to the place where she had left the traveler.

"Oh! He's gone!" she exclaimed, looking about and seeing no trace of the man. The blanket and box of food had vanished as well; there was nothing to show that an hour earlier the spring had been the center of an encampment. But Kathleen's disappointment vanished instantly as she heard the stranger's voice. "You gave me a nice fright!" he called. "What brought you back?" and looking in the direction of the sound she saw his head rising above a growth of tall brakes where he had concealed himself.

"Oh! I didn't think you'd be afraid!" she exclaimed." I only came to bring you a rug. It's mine. I can do what I like with it, and I want to give it to you," and she began hurriedly to unroll the bundle, and, holding up the rug, said: "Here it is! A pine-tree rug, to remember me by," and she ran toward the brakes to give it to her new friend, and as he reached up to take it Kathleen saw there were tears on his thin cheeks, and for a moment the little girl felt ready to cry herself. But the stranger's face brightened as he took the rug.

"Bless you, child. Now be off, and forget you ever saw me. Or rather, forget to tell of seeing me. Will you do that?" he asked eagerly.

"Not tell anyone?" she questioned. "Why not?"

"Never mind 'why not.' But do not speak of me to a living mortal. If you do I'll never see my own little girl again!" he said.

"Oh, I'll not tell. Truly I won't," Kathleen promised eagerly, "and you tell your little girl that I made the rug, and drew the pattern!"

The man nodded, as if he were almost too weary to speak, and then said: "Thank you, child. I will remember your name, and some day you shall know mine, and it may be I can be of some service to you. Now start for home, and heaven guard you," and once more his thin brown fingers clasped the little girl's hand and again he whispered: "Be off. Lose no time. Mail my letter," and sank back out of sight, and Kathleen turned and hurried down the slope wondering why the man was so fearful of discovery, and vaguely unhappy about him.

"Frisk" started along the side of the hill and made his way back to the old wagon, and once more pressing his nose against the stout gate whinnied as if demanding that it be instantly opened. Kathleen rescued her treasured hat, and, after some trouble with the homesick pony, finally succeeded in turning him toward the highway and urged him on until "Frisk" realized that he was now headed toward his new home, and once on the turnpike he trotted off so briskly that it was not long before Kathleen began to see the familiar Oak Ridge and seminary building, and the familiar buildings of the town of Gettysburg; and she remembered the letter, safe in the deep pocket of her gingham skirt, and told herself that she must ask the first person she met the way to the post-office, for Kathleen could not even imagine that she was carrying a message for one of the scouts of Lee's army, a letter directed to a trusty sympathizer with the Confederate cause, with valuable information that would be promptly forwarded to Culpeper Court House, near Lee's cavalry headquarters.

The June afternoon was drawing toward sunset when Kathleen dropped the letter into the box at Gettysburg post-office, and was now free to turn "Frisk" into the familiar road that would take her straight home. She no longer thought of even trying to visit Oak Ridge, or of searching for the lost box; she was so tired that all she could think of was getting home; and the many adventures of her long day already seemed a long way in the past as "Frisk" turned into the driveway and she saw Ted come to take the pony by the bridle.

"Well, you have made a day of it, Katy-did!" he said, as he lifted her from the saddle, "and whatever has happened to your dress and shoes?" and with his arm about his little sister Ted's surprised glance rested on the torn and untidy dress, and the muddy shoes. "Your hat seems all right, though," he added, and Kathleen, leaning against him, said: "I took it off," but in so faint a voice that Ted was instantly sure some accident had befallen her and called: "Hitty! Hitty! come here!" and Hitty came running from the kitchen with so frightened an expression that, tired though she was, Kathleen giggled in amusement and Ted exclaimed:

"Oh, it isn't the Confederate Army, Hitty; it's only Katy-did tired to death, and I reckon she fell off 'Frisk' into a mud-hole. You'd better take her in."

Kathleen was too tired to explain that she had not tumbled from the pony, and was glad enough to have the stout Hitty pick her up and carry her up-stairs to her own pleasant chamber; and, although Hitty exclaimed over the ruin of the pink gingham dress, asked reprovingly: "Whar' de worl' is dat gran' flounce?" and held up the shoes, scuffed and ruined by Kathleen's scramble at Rocky Creek, the little girl said not a word of her tremendous adventure; and not until Hitty had helped her young mistress put on a pretty blue striped dimity, fresh stockings and slippers, and was brushing the copper-colored hair, did the tired little girl speak; then she announced:

"Hitty, I gave the rug away!"

"My lan'! missy, w'ateber for?" and the amazed and disapproving Hitty stood with up-lifted hands. "An' didn' yo' tell Mistress McPherson how 'twas yo' want money for it?" she asked.

Kathleen slowly shoke her head.

"I haven't been near the McPhersons'. 'Frisk' took a wrong road, and he didn't want to come home, and—oh, everything, Hitty," Kathleen suddenly concluded, remembering that she was very nearly breaking her promise to the stranger whom, helpless and suffering, she had left on the steep slope of Rocky Creek.

"Who sum ebber *did* yo' gib dat rug?" demanded Hitty.

"To a friend of mine," Kathy responded, and the well-trained Hitty asked no more questions.

If missy wished to give the rug to a friend Hitty was sure that was far better than selling it to a stranger; and it was Hitty who explained to Mrs. Webb that the reason Missy Kathleen was so late in returning home was because the pony had taken the wrong road; and when Kathleen sat down for the belated supper she was so evidently tired out that her mother postponed questioning her; and Ted had so much to tell of the recent news of the movements of Lee's Army of Northern Virginia, whose cavalry, in a single division, was under the command of General J. E. B. Stuart, that no one gave the little girl any special notice.

It was the third day of June, 1863, and the news that Lee was concentrating his army at Culpeper had already reached Pennsylvania, and Ted now eagerly reminded his father of the May day promise that he might join the Union forces, if they would take him, if the Confederates marched into Pennsylvania.

"Wait, my boy. Lee has not yet crossed the Potomac. When he moves his columns toward the Susquehanna then we will discover if he means to attack Harrisburg, and then we'll all have to do our best to defend our homes. Governor Curtin will call for men when the Keystone State needs them," and with this Ted was forced to be satisfied, although he declared that Lee's scouts were everywhere.

"Why, Father, they travel about Pennsylvania as if they owned it! Sometimes they pretend to be farmers going to town with a wagon- load of produce, and questioning everyone they meet. I'll wager they know just where to gather in supplies for Lee's troops," said Ted, and Mr. Webb agreed, but added that he believed General Hooker, commanding the Union troops stationed on the Rappahannock, was not unmindful of Lee's movements, and that Union scouts were as active as those of the Confederates.

When Ted spoke of scouts traveling about as farmers Kathleen had looked up quickly and it flashed through her thoughts that the traveler to whom she had given her pine-tree rug might be one of those men of whom Ted spoke; then, for the first time since reaching home, she remembered the little flat package in the pocket of her gingham dress, the brass buttons, she earnestly hoped and believed, of a Union soldier. And at the thought of the buttons her fear that her new friend might be a Confederate scout vanished; she hurried through her supper and ran up-stairs to find the abused gingham dress and examine the little package. The dress was not in her room, neither was it in the closet; and Hitty was again startled and amazed when Kathleen came rushing into her kitchen demanding:

"Where *is* my pink gingham dress, Hitty Marjorum? What did you do with it?"

"My lan' ob Goshen! I didn' do nuthin' wid it," replied Hitty, rolling her eyes in a reproving glance at the excited little girl, and adding quickly: "An' yo' ain' no proper idee ob t'ings, missy! Don' yo' see dis waffle iron a-waitin', an' ain' yo' pa needin' waffles dis instant minute!" and Hitty turned toward the range as if a gingham dress was of no account in comparison with Mr. Webb's need of hot waffles.

But Kathleen was not so easily disposed of; seizing Hitty's arm she again exclaimed:

"What ever did you do with my pink gingham dress?"

"W'at I does with dat ruinated dress was ter clap it spank inter de tub an' p'oh watah on it. Dat's all, 'til I gits de chanst ter scrub it out."

Kathleen hardly waited for Hitty to finish before she dashed out of the kitchen into the adjoining shed where the tubs stood, and where the limp, soaking gingham was quickly discovered in a well- filled tub, and with a little moan of disappointment Kathleen dragged the dress to the surface and turned the pocket inside out, but the little package was gone! At this discovery Kathleen's first thought was that Hitty must have taken it out; perhaps at this moment it was safe and sound on the table in her room. But another possibility occurred to the little girl: the package might have slipped from the pocket of the dress and now be at the bottom of the tub, and at this thought Kathleen grasped the side of the wooden tub intending to tilt it sufficiently to discover if there was anything to be found. She pulled more vigorously than she intended and an instant later the tub slipped from the bench on which it stood and toppled over toward Kathleen, drenching her with water and, as she jumped backward, causing her to fall with the lurching tub nearly on top of her.

Kathleen's shrieks brought Hitty and the entire family running to the shed, but before they reached her the little girl had seen two shining golden objects drop from the tub and had managed to capture them.

CHAPTER XI

A DAY AT HOME

TED was the first one to reach the shed, and as he saw Kathleen floundering in the sweep of water from the overturned tub he exclaimed:

"Well! Katy-did it this time!" and as he lifted his sister to her feet, holding her at arm's length that her dripping garments might not touch him, he laughed heartily at her woebegone appearance, and Mrs. Webb was too anxious to get the little girl into dry garments to ask any questions as she hurried her into the house while Hitty, talking to herself and exclaiming over the flooded floor of the shed, lifted the tub back to its place.

"I didn't mean to upset it," whimpered Kathleen. "I wanted to find my pocket," and she tightly clutched the shining objects she had rescued, and as she followed her mother into her own room slipped them into a small box on the table. Mrs. Webb turned at that very moment and said:

"Kathleen! Don't touch anything until you get off those wet clothes. And I think bed is the best place for you the minute you are ready for it," and was surprised to hear Kathleen promptly agree.

"I'm 'most tired to death!" she declared, as her head touched the pillow. "I had to walk and walk," she added sleepily, and almost before her mother left the room the little girl was fast asleep.

When she awoke the next morning the June sunlight filled her room with flickering gleams, and a song-sparrow was singing about how pleasant it was to balance on the branch of an oak tree when honeysuckles and jessamine were in blossom. Kathleen's room was filled with the fragrance of early summer, and for a few moments the little girl, half awake, wondered if yesterday and all its adventures had not been a dream; then the remembrance of those queer buttons that the stranger had given her and that now rested in the drawer of her small table made the little girl spring out of bed and run across the room eager to make sure that the shining circles were really safe.

Pulling out the drawer Kathleen could hardly believe that what she saw was real; for there, shining up at her wondering gaze, were two gold pieces.

"O-ooh!" she whispered to herself. "Not buttons at all!" and she picked up one of the gold pieces as carefully as if she expected it to instantly turn into a brass button.

"Each one is five dollars!" she said; and realizing this Kathleen's first thought was that the stranger had made a mistake. "He couldn't have meant to give me so much!" the little girl told herself; and then she quickly remembered that perhaps the man, even if he did have a little girl of his own, might not know how much a little Yankee girl would value the brass buttons of a Union soldier.

"Maybe he thought five dollar gold pieces were better for a real present, and maybe he didn't have any soldier buttons to spare," she decided thoughtfully; and, although of course Kathleen could not know this, both these conclusions were right.

"I'm glad I gave him my rug," she thought, and recalling the rug Kathleen's face brightened and she began to feel as happy as the joyful song-sparrow. "It's just like a true fairy-story," she whispered, "and now I can wrap these gold pieces up in a box just as Aunty Mel did those for Janet and Beth, and I can put the box where one of them will find it! Oh, goody! goody! Oh! it's splendid," and Kathleen went hopping about the room in her bare feet feeling that all her worries were over.

"I'll ask Mother to let me visit Aunty Mel right away," she resolved as she heard Hitty coming along the passage with, as Kathleen well knew, a big pitcher full of hot water for the little girl's morning bath, and she again slipped the gold pieces back into the drawer of the table, and was as eager to prepare for breakfast as even the urgent Hitty could wish, and when a little later Mrs. Webb came into the room she found her little daughter dressed in a pretty plaided gingham and ready to go down-stairs; and Mrs. Webb smiled as Kathleen exclaimed:

"Mother! I feel just the way that bird sounds!" for the sparrow, swinging on another branch of the tall oak tree, was again singing joyfully. "I could sing all morning in the sunshine."

"That's the way I want you to feel always," Mrs. Webb said, and as with Kathleen's hand clasping her own they left the room she added: "Now tell me all about what happened yesterday!"

Kathleen stopped suddenly and her happy face clouded. She remembered that she could not tell, not even her mother, about the stranger who had a little girl, and who had fallen over the cliff at Rocky Creek.

"Oh, Mother!" she exclaimed in so woeful a tone that Mrs. Webb looked at her little daughter in surprise at the sudden change; but thinking only that Kathleen did not want to recall a clumsy fall from "Frisk's" broad back, and that she had lost her way, she did not question the little girl beyond saying:

"Well, dear, never mind; only tell me to whom you gave your rug!" and again Kathleen's half-whispered exclamation made her mother wonder if her little daughter was not more tired out by her long day's absence from home than she had realized, and as they reached the dining-room she said gently: "You can tell me about it whenever you want to, dear child. As long as you got home safely it's all right."

"And you don't feel too sorry about my tearing the flounce from my new dress, and scrubbing my shoes?" Kathleen asked eagerly; "because, truly, I couldn't help it," and her blue eyes were so earnest and pleading as she looked up into her mother's face that Mrs. Webb quickly assured her that to have her safe and happy was far more important than any dress or shoes could possibly be, and hearing this Kathleen's happy smile returned and she did not even mind Ted's teasing her about upsetting the tub on the previous night, and before breakfast was over her father and mother had promised that she might visit her Aunt Melvina the coming week.

"And I may take 'Frisk,'" she asked, "may I not? Because I want Janet and Beth to ride him, and to help me teach him tricks, like bowing and shaking hands." And, although the disapproving Hitty, standing near the door leading to the kitchen, shook her head as if to warn the entire family of the dangers of such "doings," Mr. and Mrs. Webb agreed that "Frisk" might accompany Kathleen on her visit; and now the little girl felt that all her difficulties were disappearing: she could make up the loss she had caused the Ross girls, and her mother had said that she could tell of her yesterday's adventures when she was ready to, and not before.

Kathleen resolved, however, that Aunty Mel should know about the "joke" she had planned, that she had lost the box containing the present for the twins, and had then been afraid to tell of it.

"I will surely tell her just as soon as she knows that Janet and Beth have the money," she thought. "Maybe they'll think it wasn't really lost, after all."

With Adelaide Mary for company Kathleen spent the morning in the house and garden. She had discovered a small box not unlike the one that, on her birthday morning in late April, she had taken from the table in Miss Mel's dining-room, and putting the gold pieces in this box Kathleen wrapped it in white paper and tied it securely, and then began to think of a hiding-place where it would not be discovered, and a glance at her beloved Adelaide Mary solved this difficulty. "I'll make a deep pocket in your skirt, dear Adelaide Mary," she confided to her silent friend; and Mrs. Webb seeing her small daughter happily busy with the big doll returned to her work in an upper chamber of preparing bandages and lint for the use of the field hospitals of the Union Army.

Every day brought fresh news regarding the advance of Lee's army into Northern territory. It was known that Southern resources were giving out, and that the Southern army, although paying with Confederate notes for provisions, horses and whatever they took, were determined to capture all provisions possible from the well-to-do people and fertile farms of the rich district toward which their troops were now headed.

As Mrs. Webb worked on her thoughts turned toward the gallant and loyal women of the South who, faithful to the Confederate, as she herself was to the Union cause, were working under great difficulties. She could hear Kathleen singing or talking to the faithful Adelaide Mary and Mrs. Webb sent a friendly thought to the little girls of the neighboring states, and wished with all her heart that the great nation might once more be at peace.

Sitting there in her quiet room she well knew that a tremendous battle, a battle that would mark the height of the Civil War, was near; and she feared, as did all the people along the Pennsylvania frontier, that it might come very near her own home. But Kathleen, looking forward to the delight of a visit with Aunty Mel, and resolved that Adelaide Mary should accompany her, was troubled only when she recalled the stranger helpless and alone on the slope above Rocky Creek. Then, remembering that he had been able to drag himself along the rough hillside, and that he had said in another day he would be off, the little girl's thoughts returned to the delight of Janet and Beth when they should discover the mysterious box with a five dollar gold piece for each of them.

The sound of horse's hoofs on the driveway made Kathleen look up quickly from her work of securely stitching a pocket into Adelaide Mary's silken skirt, and she had a glimpse of Ted, mounted on "Patch," as he turned into the highway and galloped off toward Gettysburg; and at that moment Hitty came toward the garden bench where Kathleen was seated.

"I'se fetched yo' a lille plate ob fresh cookies, Missy Kathy!" she smilingly announced, and Kathleen smilingly accepted the plate on which rested a half-dozen round, plump sugar cookies still warm from the oven.

"Where has Ted gone?" she asked, after politely offering Adelaide Mary a cookie, which was silently refused.

"Wal, Missy Kathy, so fur as I kin diskiver, Massa Ted has gwine ter jine de war!" replied Hitty, her face becoming very grave as she continued: "Leastways, I hears Massa Webb say sometin' like dat!"

"Oh, Hitty! Ted can't go. He isn't old enough!" declared Kathleen, jumping up from the bench, and quite forgetting both Adelaide Mary and the mulberry china plate of sugar cookies at the thought of Ted leaving home for the perils of war, and without waiting to ask any more questions the little girl ran toward the house to find her mother and discover if Ted and "Patch" were indeed off to join the Army of the Potomac.

CHAPTER XII

TROUBLE

Hitty's announcement that Ted had gone to "jine de war" was quickly explained to Kathleen, who raced up the stairs calling: "Mother! Mother! Has Ted gone to be a soldier?"

"He has gone to Gettysburg to train for service with the boys at Pennsylvania College," replied Mrs. Webb, smiling at Kathleen's anxious expression. "And he will not be at home again until we have news of the movements of the Union forces. Of course Ted is too young to be a soldier, but this training makes him happier. However, I hope it will soon be over," and Mrs. Webb's face grew sober and her smile vanished. Mr. and Mrs. Webb in giving their permission for Ted to train with the college boys could not realize that within a month fifty-seven students from Pennsylvania College, together with four from the seminary and twenty two other youths of the town would be members of an "emergency infantry," in Company A, Pennsylvania, and fighting almost at the thresholds of their own homes; and that Ted, young as he was, was to prove himself a worthy soldier.

"He didn't tell me good-bye," complained Kathleen, and then, recalling the pleasant fact that in a few days she would begin her visit with Aunt Mel, she added quickly: "Perhaps I'll see him when I am at Aunty Mel's."

"Why, I would not be surprised," agreed Mrs. Webb, and remembering the deserted cookies on the garden bench Kathleen fled back to pick up the big doll, make sure the little white box was safe in Adelaide Mary's pocket, and then to sit down contentedly and enjoy Hitty's delicious cookies.

The Webb farm lay on a pleasant slope, and from the garden bench Kathleen could look off to the distant heights of Blue Ridge Mountains. Toward the east rose Cemetery Ridge, and nearer at hand a wooded hill towered above the surrounding country. Looking at this hill Kathleen wondered why it had no name. From its northern side a bold shoulder stood out, the "Little Round Top," where in the battle of Gettysburg Brigadier-General Weed was to die in its defense.

But there was no thought of possible battles in Kathleen's mind that June morning as she sat in the pleasant garden eating sugar cookies and looking out over the pleasant countryside, and planning all the good times that she was so soon to enjoy with Janet and Beth Ross, and she was eager to tell Aunt Mel the story of the lost box. In spite of all these pleasant possibilities, there was, however, a little shadowy worry in Kathleen's thoughts when she remembered that her adventure at Rocky Creek was a secret; she wanted to tell her mother and father all about it: to repeat what the stranger had said of her courage, of his own little girl, and to show them the gold pieces, and Kathleen sighed as she whispered to herself:

"Maybe I can't ever tell them. Not unless the stranger comes to see us and says that I may. Perhaps he will come!" and at this thought the little girl's face brightened. Anyway, she reflected, Janet and Beth would have the gold pieces, and watching two wide-winged gold and bronze butterflies fluttering over the syringa bushes, listening to a bright breasted cardinal singing "Pret-*tee! pretty! pretty!*" Kathleen's shadowy troubles disappeared, and she and Adelaide Mary carried the mulberry plate to Hitty's kitchen for a fresh supply of cookies and a glass of cool milk.

The day set for Kathleen's ride to Aunty Mel's proved to be exactly the right day to ride "Frisk" to Gettysburg; and, wearing her riding dress of blue linen and sailor hat of blue straw with a broad white ribbon band, Kathleen carrying Adelaide Mary came running to the yard where "Frisk," all saddled and bridled, awaited her.

Mr. and Mrs. Webb, seated in the comfortable Concord wagon, with Kathleen's small square trunk in the back, and drawn by one of the fine farm horses, were going with the little girl, and Kathleen mounted the pony and kept pace beside the wagon smiling her pleasure in having her plans so happily accomplished. Here she was, she reflected, mounted on "Frisk" and bound for her aunt's with Adelaide Mary securely seated just in front of her with the little box for the Ross girls safe in the doll's pocket.

It seemed to the little girl that the fields and hills had never been as beautiful as this June morning. The wide spreading field of wheat past which the road led, the blues of the distant mountains, and the fragrance of many blossoms made it indeed a scene of peace and beauty; but even as Kathleen rode so gaily, marching armies along highways and mountain passes were moving toward these wooded slopes and open fields where gallant Confederate and brave Union soldiers were soon to meet in an historic battle.

Miss Melvina gave her guests the warmest of welcomes. She was always delighted to have Kathleen visit her, and now declared that Kathleen must stay until after July 4th, and Mrs. Webb gave her consent.

"But Kathleen must promise not to start out alone with 'Frisk,'" she added, telling of Kathleen's long day's absence from home, and Miss Mel and the little girl both promptly assured her that Kathleen would not go out on "Frisk" without a companion.

"General Hooker is moving the Union army northward to guard Washington," Kathleen heard her father say, and her Aunt Mel's quick response:

"And Lee knows that, as well as all the resources of this part of the world, for his scouts are everywhere. It is said one of them fell over a bluff at Rocky Creek last week, but managed to get off and took two fine horses from a farm near by with him; but he left a roll of Confederate money to pay for them."

"O-ooh!" whispered Kathleen, who was instantly sure that this Confederate scout must be the stranger to whom she had given her pine-tree rug, and whose gold pieces were at that very moment safe in the pocket of Adelaide Mary's silken skirt; and Kathleen suddenly recalled how many questions the stranger had asked her, and her face flushed uncomfortably as she remembered that she had told the man that her father had four horses, and that many of the neighboring farmers had fine young horses, and many cattle; and Kathleen began to feel herself almost a traitor to the cause of the Union, for which Ted was so eager to fight, as she heard her father say:

"There are rumors that this scout must have had friends in Gettysburg, who probably told him just where to look for good horses and fat cattle;" and at this Kathleen sobbed aloud.

"Why, Kathleen! Whatever is the matter?" exclaimed her mother, putting her arm about the unhappy child, while her Aunt Mel looked at the little girl in surprise.

"I believe I frightened the child with all this talk of scouts and battles," declared Mr. Webb, "but we must face the fact that both Northern and Southern armies are marching in this direction, and that before many weeks will meet in battle."

But this was small comfort to Kathleen. "Oh, dear! oh, dear!" she continued to sob, all her happy plans quite forgotten until Aunt Mel exclaimed:

"Here come Janet and Beth!" and at this Kathleen choked back her sobs, hastily wiped away her tears and was able to smile as she greeted the delighted twins who at once began to ask about "Frisk" and "Patch," and exclaimed over Adelaide Mary, whom Kathleen still held in her arms.

"May I not take her?" asked Beth, reaching out her arms for the doll, quite sure that Kathleen would be as pleased to share the doll's company as Beth was eager to enjoy it. But Kathleen drew back quickly, taking a firmer hold than ever on Adelaide Mary's unyielding form.

"Don't touch her!" she exclaimed, in so sharp a voice that Beth and Janet both stared at her in amazement, for the twins had never before known Kathleen to be anything but friendly and unselfish, and Beth's round face grew sober and Janet clasped her sister's plump little hand and whispered:

"Never mind, Beth; it's Kathleen's doll."

"Of course it's my doll!" exclaimed Kathleen, and when I want you to play with her I'll tell you," and, hardly realizing what she said or did the unhappy Kathleen turned and ran out of the room, leaving the astonished twins staring after her as, hand in hand, they stood near the door that opened into Miss Melvina's garden where Mr. and Mrs. Webb and Miss Melvina were talking together.

"Maybe we'd better go home," said Janet, and Beth nodded silently, and still hand-in-hand the two little girls started down the garden path, but Miss Melvina ran after them.

"Wherever are you going, girls? And where is Kathleen? Did you not understand that I wanted you to have dinner with us?" she questioned, as she smiled down at the sober faces of her little neighbors.

"Thank you very much, Miss Mel; but we must go home," Janet managed to say; for it was always Janet who seemed the elder of the two, while Beth was sure whatever Janet decided must be right.

"Oh! that's too bad. Poor Kathleen will be disappointed; she has her doll, and was planning a fine time with you this afternoon," said Miss Melvina, and then her face grew serious, for poor little Beth at the mention of Kathleen's doll had begun to sniff, and tears were now rolling down her round cheeks.

"Why, Beth, dear!" and instantly Miss Melvina's arms were about the little girl. "Do tell me what the matter is."

"Kathleen doesn't like us any more. She don't want us!" sobbed Beth.

CHAPTER XIII

KATHLEEN DISAPPEARS

KATHLEEN fled through the house to the back yard, raced across this toward the stables and, hardly noticing her pony's welcoming whinny, stood for a moment looking about the big cool barn whose doors, open on each end, gave a view of Gettysburg on one side and of Seminary Ridge on the other, and as her glance rested on the cupola of the seminary building she remembered that she had told the stranger that from this cupola one could see South Mountain, and many of the roads leading from Gettysburg toward the west, south-west and northwest; and, remembering Aunt Mel's declaration that the Confederate scouts were seeking not only supplies for Lee's army but a gathering place for his scattered troops Kathleen again told herself that if the Confederates came to Gettysburg she had told their scout the very best place from which to watch for the advance of the Union forces.

"Oh, dear!" she whispered. "What can I do? I wish the Union Army would come first. I wish I could do

125

something to help President Lincoln. I wish——"
but the sound of voices made Kathleen look about
a little fearfully, for she was too troubled and
unhappy to want anyone to find her just then and,
noticing a ladder against a haymow, she hurriedly
scrambled up and quickly concealed herself in the
heaped up hay, and had hardly settled herself
before two men entered the barn, and without a
suspicion that their conversation could be overheard began to talk excitedly.

"I tell you Lee's army is already in Pennsylvania,"
said one. "And I'll wager someone in our very town
helped that scout get away from Rocky Creek," and
hearing this Kathleen held her hand firmly across
her mouth, fearful that she might call out that she
had not known the friendly stranger was an enemy to
the Union.

"Well," said another voice, "I'm off within an hour
to Harrisburg to join the militia, or I'd take my
chances on trying to reach General Hooker and let
him know that Lee's men are on the march toward
Chambersburg."

"Where'd you find Hooker?" questioned the first
speaker scornfully, and Kathleen forgot her fear of
discovery and leaned so far forward to hear the man's
reply that a bunch of loose hay tumbled from the

mow and the surprised men looked up to see a small girl, holding a big doll, peering at them with startled eyes over the edge of the haymow!

"Great Scott! I thought we'd been overheard by some lurking scout!" declared the last speaker, and both men laughed in relief to find that only a small girl and her doll, no doubt playing "house," they thought, had overheard their conversation.

"Where is General Hooker?" demanded Kathleen, and at her serious voice both men laughed again, and one of them said:

"It's said he crossed the Potomac on Thursday the 25th; to-day is Saturday the 27th and he must be near Harper's Ferry."

"Harper's Ferry," repeated the little girl, soberly, and at this both the men laughed again, and the man said:

"Maybe you'd like to carry a message to the Union Army to hurry up a bit? I reckon you wouldn't have to go as far as Harper's Ferry. But I must be off. You are Miss Melvina's niece, the little Yankee Girl?" he added, and Kathleen managed to reply: "Yes, sir!" and the men, one of whom had been employed by Miss Melvina, now hurried away, and in an instant Kathleen was making her way down the ladder resolved that she would be the messenger to warn the Union general that Lee's army was advancing into Pennsylvania.

"I must leave the box for Janet and Beth," she thought, and pulled out the threads that fastened the pocket in Adelaide Mary's skirt and took out the small package; and now a new resolve came into her mind: to also leave Adelaide Mary for the twins. "Then Beth will know I didn't mean to be hateful," she thought, suddenly recalling Beth's surprised and unhappy expression when she had refused to let her take the doll.

"I mustn't let anyone see me," Kathleen whispered to herself; for she knew she could not possibly explain why she wanted to be of help to the Union Army, for that would mean telling of the aid she had given to a Confederate scout.

"I must help Ted's army some way!" she thought unhappily, feeling this was all she could do to make up for her innocent disloyalty, and creeping along close to a stone wall that separated her aunt's field from the one in which the Ross cottage stood.

It was now noon, and there was no one to be seen when Kathleen, leaving the shelter of the wall, ran quickly toward the cottage and, giving Adelaide Mary a parting hug, set the doll on the front door-step sure that the twins would promptly discover her.

"Now where will I put the package?" she thought, looking about to make sure that she was not seen. "Maybe 'twill be better just to drop it in the path," she decided, and this she did, and, with one more glance toward Adelaide Mary, Kathleen fled back to the shelter of the stone wall and ran along until out of sight of the cottage; then crossing an open field she came out on the highway and for a moment stood looking about uncertain which direction to take. Toward the south was the town of Gettysburg, and beyond it she could see Cemetery Hill.

"I wonder which road leads to Harper's Ferry?" she said aloud, and then, believing that she very soon would meet someone to tell her the way, and confident that the wide road on which she stood really did lead in the direction she wished to take, Kathleen started off at a good pace.

In the meantime Miss Melvina had comforted Beth, and convinced Janet that Kathleen would be sadly disappointed not to see them at luncheon.

"And after lunch I know she wants you to help her teach 'Frisk,'" said Aunt Mel; "she will be here in a little while to make friends. I am sure she will!"

Beth and Janet were quite ready to be comforted, and as Miss Melvina walked between them back to the house the twins were again smiling and happy and ready to believe that Kathleen had not meant to be unkind. Remembering all Kathleen's eager generosity toward them it was very easy for Janet and Beth to feel sure that Kathleen had some reason for refusing to let Beth take the doll; as indeed she had, for Kathleen had feared that Beth might discover the package concealed in the doll's pocket.

No one felt at all troubled by the fact that Kathleen had disappeared; both Mrs. Webb and Miss Melvina believed that Kathleen, ashamed of her rudeness toward Beth, had gone to her room and that she would soon reappear quite ready to make friends with the twins.

Even when Dosia had rung the bell and all the others were in the dining-room and Kathleen did not come no one was anxious; there were no dangers to fear for her, and when Mrs. Webb ran up to the room that Kathleen was to occupy and did not find her she only believed that her little daughter was grieved and ashamed and did not want to come to the dining-room, and so told the others that luncheon was not to wait.

"Kathleen cannot be far off," she said on entering the dining- room, "and very likely will appear before luncheon is over;" and they all took their seats and Miss Mel had just spoken of Ted and wished that he might be one of the party when Beth exclaimed:

"Oh! Here he is; on 'Patch,' coming up the drive," and a moment later Ted, wearing the blue uniform of a Union soldier, appeared in the doorway and smilingly saluted the company, and in the surprise of his unexpected appearance Kathleen was forgotten until, half-way through luncheon, Ted exclaimed:

"Where's Katy-did? and how long a visit will she make this time?"

"She is to stay until July 4th; and you'll see her, I expect, in a few moments," replied his mother.

"I hope so; for I'm a soldier now, and with the Confederates headed this way Gettysburg is sure to see trouble, and I'll not come visiting again for some time," he responded soberly, and in answering his father's questions regarding the preparations being made to defend the town Kathleen was again forgotten, so that no search was made for her until well on in the afternoon when Ted was obliged to leave without having seen her, and then it was discovered that Janet and Beth had also vanished.

"Very likely they are with Kathleen playing some game," suggested Mr. Webb, as the time for him and Mrs. Webb to start for their home drew near, and, although they were sorry to go without seeing Kathleen, her father and mother had no thought but what their little daughter was with the twins and not far away, and set off for home thinking of the marching armies that every hour were advancing toward them, and more troubled by this than by any fear regarding Kathleen.

It was not until late in the afternoon that Miss Melvina decided to go to the Ross cottage and walk home with Kathleen who, she confidently believed, was there with the twins; and as she approached the house she saw Beth on the front door-step with Adelaide Mary in her arms, and at this Miss Mel smiled approvingly.

"That is just what Kathleen would do: bring her doll to Beth," she thought, and when Janet came running to meet her exclaiming: "Oh! Miss Mel! Miss Mel! We have found the lost box! The one you meant to give us, with the two gold pieces in it," she was too much surprised to even wonder why Kathleen was not with the twins; and not until Janet had told of finding the little package "right in the path," and both the girls had joyfully thanked Miss Mel, did she look about expectantly for her little niece.

"Where is Kathleen?" she asked, and the twins stared at her wonderingly, and not until Miss Melvina repeated her question did Janet reply:

"We don't know. We haven't seen her."

"But the doll? Where did Adelaide Mary come from?" she asked.

"When we got home the doll was here sitting right against the door," Beth explained eagerly, "and we have been expecting Kathleen ever since," she added.

"She must be at home after all," said Miss Mel; and, puzzled by the unexplained appearance of the missing box, and a little troubled that Kathleen had hidden herself during Ted's visit, Miss Melvina bade the twins good-bye and started toward home.

Dosia declared that Missy Kathy had not been seen, and a thorough search of the house, garden and stable revealed no trace of the missing girl.

"If 'Frisk' was missing I should believe Kathleen had started for home; but he's safe in his stall. Whatever can have befallen the child?" said Miss Melvina, more frightened than she dared own even to herself by the fact that the little girl could not be found.

CHAPTER XIV

KATHLEEN RETURNS

WHEN evening deepened and Kathleen had not been found Miss Mclvina sent a messenger to the Webb farm, hoping that the little girl might be safe in her own home.

Mr. and Mrs. Webb could hardly believe it possible that their little daughter was lost; and Mr. Webb returned with the messenger to Miss Melvina's, promising to send Mrs. Webb word the moment Kathleen was found.

But Sunday morning, June 28th, 1863, dawned without news of the missing girl. It was on this day that Major-General George Gordon Meade received the news that he had been appointed commander of the Union Army. He was a Pennsylvanian, and now was to defend his own state; and, although uncertain as to the enemy's movements, Meade continued to move the army northward.

That day and the following were days of deep trouble and anxiety for the Webbs and for Miss Melvina, for Kathleen had not returned nor were they able to discover any trace of her. Janet and Beth guarded

Adelaide Mary as carefully as if she were the most valuable possession in the world, and both the little girls went about with sober faces, wondering and fearful about their missing friend.

Aunt Dosia, however, declared there was no need to worry about Kathleen. "Dese are war times, Miss Mel; an' bein' war times 'tain' likely dat de folks whar' Missy Kathy is kin fin' de way ter sen' her home. Dat's all. *She's* all right." And all Kathleen's relatives could do now was to hope and pray that the negro woman was right, and that Kathleen was indeed with friendly people who would guard and care for her. For now, on the night of June 30th, Confederate troops from the west, from the north, and from the east were hurrying along the roads leading to "the hub of the wheel." And Meade's forces were also marching on toward Gettysburg, and the two armies were soon to meet in one of the greatest battles of history; for, at five o'clock on the morning of July 1st, 1863, three miles from Gettysburg on the road to Cashtown, a Union soldier, Corporal Alpheus Hodges, in charge of the Union picket outpost, fired his carbine to warn that the Confederates were approaching, and the terrible battle that was to rage over the countryside for three days had begun.

From the cupola of the seminary building, where Kathleen had looked happily out over a peaceful scene, the gallant Union General Buford directed the opening battle, and the Confederates, under General Hill, were advancing along the Chambersburg turnpike. On that day the Union cause was to lose one of its finest generals, Major-General John Fulton Reynolds, a native of Pennsylvania.

Janet and Beth nearly forgot Kathleen as, staying closely indoors with their mother, they looked from the upper windows to watch the long grey columns of the Southern troops, and to exclaim over the marching Union soldiers in blue. Adelaide Mary, carefully held by Janet, gazed out as if seeking the missing Kathleen, and saw the Union forces give way before the matchless troops under General Hill and Ewell and pressed back into the town of Gettysburg, where hundreds were made prisoners. And now for two days the town was in the hands of the Confederates; but the people remained in their homes undisturbed, and but few houses were injured by the shot and shell that were hurled over the town.

Ted was one of the first to be taken prisoner, and as he saw his valued "Patch" driven off by a dashing young Confederate soldier it was difficult for the boy to keep back his tears and to remember that he was a Union soldier. He knew of Kathleen's disappearance, and with the entire countryside given over to battle Ted feared that his little sister might never be heard from; where he would be taken he could not imagine. One of his guards, Ted noticed, was lame. This man, tall and thin with deep-set dark eyes, was called "Rob" by his companions and was evidently a person of some importance.

"Your name, young Yankee?" he demanded of Ted, and when the boy responded: "Theodore Webb, Junior," it seemed to Ted that the dark eyes rested on him with a keener interest, and "Rob" asked: "Only son?" in a more gentle tone.

Ted nodded, and was surprised when the man continued: "Any sisters?"

But at this question Ted's courage faltered as he remembered that he could do nothing for his little sister, who, he felt sure, must be wandering among unnumbered dangers, and he replied: "One, Kathleen! And she is lost," in so broken a voice that the dark-eyed Confederate looked at him pitifully as he exclaimed:

"Lost? That child has not been wandering about all this time? Didn't she reach home safely?" and at these questions it was Ted's turn to be surprised and to question in his turn:

"Have you seen her? A little girl with blue eyes and yellow hair? A little girl eleven years old, and always smiling?" and at Ted's description of his sister "Rob" smiled as he responded:

"When did you last see her?"

"I haven't seen her for weeks. But she was at Aunt Mel's on Saturday, and no one has seen her since; and this raging battle from Cemetery Hill to Oak Ridge——" and again the boy's voice faltered. Instantly a friendly hand rested on his shoulder, and Ted looked up to find the dark eyes of his guard resting kindly upon him, and heard a friendly voice say:

"Don't be troubled about your sister. I'll do my best to get news of her and let you know. Very likely she is in some farmhouse near by."

"Thank you," stammered the surprised Ted, wondering why this lame soldier should try to help either him or Kathleen.

That night, waiting for a fresh encounter, both armies rested on their arms; and in the late evening Ted found the friendly guard again beside him bringing him food and drink, and again bidding him not to worry about Kathleen.

The morning of Thursday, July 2nd, 1863, passed without any fighting, except occasional shots along the skirmish line. Along those pleasant country slopes and wooded hills, on Seminary Ridge, on the height of Round Top, at the Peach Orchard, and along the stone walls and quiet roads, where only a few weeks earlier Kathleen had rode "Frisk" in perfect security, were now massed Union troops under Major-General Daniel E. Sickles, and General Humphreys; and early in the day their commanding officer, General Meade, quietly appeared at Cemetery Ridge, his long-bearded, haggard face worn and tired after a sleepless night. Officers and men crowded about him, encouraged by his serious, businesslike air.

From early afternoon until darkness blotted out field and hill the dreadful battle went on with terrible losses on both sides, General Meade, in the midst of the fighting, proving himself equal to the command of his army, as the Confederates led by the gallant Longstreet crowded forward up the slopes of Round Top, only to be driven back.

On Friday morning, July 3rd, 1863, the conflict raged along the intervale near Rocky Creek, in front of that very cliff down which the scout, "Rob," had tumbled, and up which Kathleen had so courageously climbed to his assistance. The hot July sun beat down upon brave men marching to their death, General Pickett's wonderful Confederate soldiers left "an immortal record of their gallantry and their willingness to die at Lee's bidding."

The three days' battle of Gettysburg closed in front of Big Round Top. Lee was obliged to retreat, and before noon on Saturday, July 4th, 1863, his army was moving down the Chambersburg and Fairfield roads. At nightfall, under cover of night and a heavy rainfall, Lee's defeated army had left Gettysburg, and Pennsylvania was no longer in danger of capture by the Confederates.

Ted, under guard with other Union captives, that night again found the lame guard "Rob" marching beside him, and heard him whisper: "Could you find your way home from here?"

"Sure!" Ted answered briefly.

"Then good-bye, and good luck to you. My name is Robert Summers. Your small sister did me a big service at Rocky Creek; tell her I'll not forget it; and her pine-tree rug has started for Georgia!"

"'Pine-tree rug'?" echoed the puzzled Ted.

"She'll tell you about it. She's safe with her aunt. But fall out; drop by the roadside, and get home as best you may," commanded the guard, and Ted found himself suddenly pushed into the underbrush where he lay fearful and trembling as the line of Union prisoners were hurried forward through the rain of the summer night.

He scrambled over the rough ground until the sound of the marching troops grew faint, and his fears of being recaptured vanished, and found himself near a slow moving stream.

"This must be Marsh Creek," he whispered to himself, and too tired to take another step the boy soldier crept close to the trunk of a fallen oak tree and, in spite of rain and all the possibilities of danger near at hand, he was almost instantly asleep and did not awake until sunrise the next morning.

Ted never liked to speak to anyone of his journey over Seminary Ridge to reach Aunt Mel's on that Sunday morning after the Battle of Gettysburg. Every hill and dale, every rock and rill marked the history of tragic deeds, and when the boy came in sight of his aunt's peaceful home, standing as quiet and secure as he remembered it, he gave a little shout of delight and raced down the road forgetting all the horrors of war and eager to be again at home.

Kathleen, on the porch with Janet and Beth and Adelaide Mary, was the first one to discover that the hurrying boy in blue was the missing Ted, for whom at that very moment his father was searching among the wounded soldiers who were being cared for in every farmhouse and in field hospitals near by.

"Well, Katy-did! Your friend, the Confederate scout, sent me home!" declared Ted, as Kathleen threw her arms about him, crying: "Ted! dear Ted," over and over, until Aunty Mel and Mrs. Webb came hurrying from the upper chambers where wounded soldiers were sheltered, to take their part in rejoicing over Ted's safety, and his escape from the Confederates.

CHAPTER XV

KATHLEEN'S FRIENDS

TED was eager to hear of Kathleen's adventures; and that afternoon stretched out on the broad sofa in Aunt Mel's cool sitting-room, with Kathleen busily winding bandages as she sat beside him in a wicker rocking-chair, the little girl told him all that had befallen her, beginning with her encounter with the scout, his accident and the help she had given him.

"Lucky for me, Katy-did, that you didn't desert him. I'll wager neither of us would be here safe and sound if you had not helped him. But what did he mean about the 'pine-tree rug'?" questioned Ted; and in answering that question Kathleen had to go back to her birthday, and the amazed Ted listened to the story of the lost box intended for Janet and Beth, Kathleen's efforts to earn enough money to replace the gold pieces intended for the twins, and the gift of the Confederate scout that had enabled her to do this.

"And don't you remember when I pulled the tub of water over on me?" asked Kathleen, and Ted laughingly replied that he should never forget it.

"Well, my dress was in that tub, and I'd forgotten to take the gold pieces out of the pocket," explained Kathleen, and then began the story of her adventures during the time she had been missing.

"Those men in Aunt Mel's barn said someone ought to let the Union generals know that Lee's army was marching this way," she began, "and I thought even a little girl could do that; and I'd just heard about a Confederate scout at Rocky Creek——"

"Our friend," interrupted Ted, and Kathleen nodded, and there was a brief silence and then she went on: "Well, I thought I ought to do something just as quick as I could to make up for telling a Confederate scout all about the places he wanted to know," and she looked at Ted questioningly, and this time it was Ted who nodded, and the little girl continued: "I walked and walked, but I didn't meet anyone to tell me the way to Harper's Ferry, and when I came to a lane leading to a farmhouse I went in to ask, and the woman wouldn't let me go out again. She said there were Confederate soldiers in Chambersburg, and that I'd have to stay with her until my own folks came to fetch me; and then General Lee came——"

"What?" exclaimed the astonished Ted, sitting up and looking at his small sister as if sure that he had not heard correctly. "Do you mean to say you were at

General Robert Lee's headquarters all through the battle of Gettysburg?"

"I guess so. Anyway I saw him; and I like him and I won't ever forget him," Kathleen replied solemnly, "and when my scout came after me,"——and at this statement Ted again exclaimed in surprise, and Kathleen nodded, and continued: "Yes, my scout came after me yesterday morning before daylight, and he brought me all the way to Aunt Mel's front door; and I like him, and I like General Lee, and they are both my friends," Kathleen concluded bravely.

"That's a pretty thing for a Yankee girl to say," declared Ted; but nevertheless he knew that the lame Confederate soldier had indeed proven himself a loyal friend to the Yankee girl and to her soldier brother.

Kathleen made no reply; she was thinking of a promise the Confederate scout had made her. He had said: "When the pine-tree rug reaches my little girl she will write you a letter. Her name is Claudia Summers," and Kathleen, in her turn, had eagerly promised to answer any letter that she might receive from the little Confederate girl.

It was nearly a week later when Mr. and Mrs. Webb, with Kathleen seated between them, and Ted, mounted on "Frisk," trotting along beside them, started for their own home, leaving the battle-field of

Gettysburg behind them. For, although the armies
of the contending forces had occupied many miles of
the surrounding countryside, the ridges beyond the
town had been the central points of the battles
where General Lee's forces of 78,000 soldiers had
been defeated by Meade's troops that numbered
94,000 men.

The Webbs were eager to be once more at home,
but Ted's thoughts dwelt unhappily on his lost
horse, "Patch"; and as Hitty came running to welcome them, the boy urged the pony on to the stable
while his father and mother and Kathleen all
endeavored to answer Hitty's excited questions and
to assure her that her own "Mammy Dosia" was
safe and unharmed.

As Ted unsaddled "Frisk," a familiar whinny made
him start suddenly. "Sounded like 'Patch,'" he
thought mournfully, quite sure such thing could not
be possible; but a second whinny made him turn
quickly toward the box stall which "Patch" had
always occupied, and with an exclamation of delight
the boy rushed toward it and exclaiming: "'Patch!
Patch!'" he pushed open the stall door and throwing
his arms about the neck of the grey horse, hugged
"Patch" delightedly.

"My lan'! I s'pected yo' was all dade!" Hitty
announced as she helped carry Kathleen's trunk up

to the little girl's room. "W'en de grey hoss came a-racin' inter de ya'd I says——"

"'The grey horse!' Oh, Hitty! *Is* 'Patch' here?" exclaimed Kathleen, who had just established Adelaide Mary in her accustomed corner, and now turned eagerly toward Hitty.

"Yas'm, Missy Kathy: de grey hoss has bin h'ar nigh a week! How come yo' all, an' my mammy, wan' kilt?" demanded Hitty, but Kathleen was already racing off toward the stable to rejoice with Ted over the return of "Patch." Ted wondered what fate had befallen the young Confederate soldier who had taken the grey horse on that first day of battle when Gettysburg had been in the hands of the Confederates; and the Yankee boy, grateful for his own escape from wounds or imprisonment, and rejoicing in this unexpected good fortune of "Patch's" return, no longer cherished ill-will against the Southern lad who, for all Ted knew, might now be lying dead on the field of battle.

Kathleen rejoiced to be once more in her own home, and when her father and mother listened to the story of their little daughter's adventures, beginning on that June day when she had ridden off on "Frisk" with the pine-tree rug tied to her saddle, they felt that fortune had indeed befriended their little daughter, and their soldier son who, but for the friendship of the Confederate scout, might at this moment be a prisoner of the defeated Confederates.

Ted was full of eager praise for the great generals who had led the Union forces to victory, and he proudly declared that Pennsylvania, the Keystone State, had furnished the heroes of the battle of Gettysburg.

"Listen!" he demanded excitedly; "didn't General Meade command the army? And didn't General Reynolds fall in battle on the first day? And didn't General Winfield Scott Hancock direct and rally the troops, and command the line of battle on the second day? And they are all Pennsylvanians."

"And there were many more brave Pennsylvanians in battle," agreed Mr. Webb. "And their services to their state will not be forgotten," and as his glance rested on Ted the boy realized his father was proud indeed that his own son had been one of the defenders of Gettysburg.

Kathleen had listened in silence; thanks to the care and kindness of the Confederate officers who been stationed at the farmhouse where she found shelter, the little Yankee girl had been shielded from the dreadful sights of the terrible battles that had raged so near. And now remembering the imposing figure of the great soldier General Robert E. Lee, the gentle glance of the brown eyes that had rested so kindly upon her, she exclaimed:

"They weren't any braver than General Lee! And he didn't care if I was a little Yankee girl; he liked me just the same."

"There! That's the way she talks, Father!" said Ted accusingly. "She's a great Yankee girl to be praising Confederate generals."

"Brave Americans, just the same, my boy," Mr. Webb reminded him, and Ted said no more; he had seen the heroic spectacle of the advancing Confederate ranks of Pickett and Pettigrew; he knew of the valor of Longstreet and Sorrel, and owned to himself that his father was right, and after that whenever Kathleen spoke of General Lee as her friend Ted made no complaint.

Although Adelaide Mary had been tenderly cared for by Janet and Beth, Kathleen decided that it was time her treasured doll had an entirely new wardrobe; and as Janet and Beth were coming to the Webb farm for a visit in August she resolved that Adelaide Mary should surprise the visitors by appearing in a new dress and hat.

"Her things shall all be white," thought Kathleen, "and her skirt shall have little ruffles all over it!" and Mrs. Webb promised that a trunk in the attic, which

Kathleen knew contained all sorts of treasures, should be opened for Kathleen to select materials for Adelaide Mary's new hat and dress.

"May I have anything I want from that trunk?" the little girl asked, and her mother smilingly promised:

"Yes, anything you want," and the next morning Kathleen climbed the attic stairs and made her way to the small black leather-covered trunk that stood near a window.

She knew that this trunk held rolls of cloth, bits of silk, and some partly worn garments, and Kathleen was sure she could find in it exactly what she wanted for her doll's dress.

CHAPTER XVI

A GOLDEN GOWN

THE attic window was open; and, before looking into the treasured trunk, Kathleen seated herself on a low box near the window, and looked out across the peaceful fields toward the ledges where she liked so much to play.

The July day was warm and fragrant with the midsummer sweetness of ripening grains, and Kathleen's thoughts went back to the May baskets for Janet and Beth that she had concealed among the tall ferns at the foot of the ledge, and she recalled the conversation she had then overheard between two Confederate scouts, and a little smile crept over Kathleen's face as she remembered that her father had said that it was fortunate she had kept so quiet and had remembered what the strangers had said regarding the northward movements of the Confederate forces because he could now warn Gettysburg to prepare to meet invasion; and she remembered the young Union soldier, Mason, who had shared the May day supper, and that he had declared Kathleen's news would be of the greatest help to the Union Army, and that because of Kathleen's news he had hurried off, eager to carry it to the commanding officer of the Northern Army.

"And maybe that helped, after all," Kathleen thought wistfully; for the little girl, in spite of the good fortune that had come to her and to Ted through her meeting with the Confederate scout, could not forget that she had been the one who had thoughtlessly told of horses, cattle, and of stores of shoes and supplies that the enemy's forces had promptly secured. The little girl never wholly forgot this fact, and for the remainder of her life Kathleen was never very ready to confide in anyone; and now she was comforted and reassured by recalling that Mason had felt her message of importance and had praised her for remembering so exactly what she had overheard.

"And I did see General Lee," she thought, with a little smile at the memory of the great general's kindly words to the little Yankee girl who had wandered into the very headquarters of the advancing Confederates.

Turning from the window Kathleen lifted the lid of the trunk, and, kneeling before it, drew out the folds of paper so carefully tucked over its contents; then she gave a little exclamation of delight, for the first thing her glance rested on was a strip of silvery blue silk, and she could instantly imagine the beautiful cape it would make for Adelaide Mary, and held it up that she might admire the interwoven colors that gave the material its changing hues.

"That will be splendid!" she declared aloud; "and there is enough for a cape and a bonnet," and she laid the silk on the floor beside her and again turned to the trunk, drawing out small neatly rolled packages of material left from her own and her mother's dresses, and selecting bits here and there of pretty muslin or bright-colored wool until she had a fine supply from which to replenish her doll's wardrobe.

And now she came to another layer of folded paper, and lifting this Kathleen stared in amazement; for there, neatly folded, lay the most wonderful dress Kathleen had ever beheld. It was the color of ripen ing corn, and the little girl felt as if the trunk had suddenly been one filled with sunlight; and as she carefully lifted the long treasured gown, which Mrs. Webb's grandmother had brought from Italy half a century ago, the dim attic room seemed to glow and shimmer from its golden beauty.

"It's brocade!" Kathleen whispered, holding up the dress whose soft folds now showed dim patterns of sprays of wheat, and of a trailing vine whose tiny leaves seemed of pure gold.

"It's lovely! It's like a fairy dress," thought Kathleen, spreading out the long full skirt, and admiring the short bodice and flowing sleeves. "Mother said I could have anything in the black trunk," she whispered, and wondered what Mrs. Webb would say if her small daughter should suddenly appear wearing this splendid dress.

"I'll dress up and s'prise her!" she resolved, and glancing back into the trunk she gave another exclamation for there lay a hat as beautiful as the dress. It was gold-colored straw, and about its high crown rested a white plume.

"Oh!" exclaimed the delighted girl, gently lifting the hat and instantly placing it on her own head, and then looking eagerly around wishing the attic had a mirror so she might see if this tall-crowned golden hat had not instantly changed her into a grown-up lady; but the attic had not even a broken mirror, and Kathleen turned again to the trunk. "I guess this is all," she said, seeing only a folded black garment; lifting this it proved to be a long cape of dull black satin.

"That would cover the dress all up," she thought, but at that moment Ted called to her from the foot of the attic stairs: "Katy-did? Katy-did? Come on out

THERE LAY A HAT AS BEAUTIFUL AS THE DRESS

to the pasture and we'll give 'Frisk' his first lesson," and in an instant Kathleen had bundled the golden dress and hat back into the trunk and was running down the stairs and off to the pasture with Ted.

"Frisk" was feeding quietly not far from the pasture bars, and did not even lift his head when Kathleen called: "Frisk! Frisk!" But Ted's little grey horse at the first sight of his master gave his usual welcoming whinny and came trotting toward them.

"I wish 'Frisk' would do this," said Kathleen, as "Patch" bowed so low that his thick mane nearly touched the ground.

"He will just as soon as he knows you want him to," said Ted, giving "Patch" a young tender carrot as a reward for his good manners; and then seeing the pony had turned toward them, called: "Come on, 'Frisk.' Here's one for you," and held out another toward the pony who came slowly toward them as if uncertain as to what might befall him. But he nibbled the carrot gratefully, and whinnied expectantly hoping for more, while "Patch" rested his head on Ted's shoulder as if looking on in amusement.

"Always give him a reward: carrots, an apple, sugar; whatever you find he likes best," said Ted as he began to teach "Frisk" to bend his head in response to the command: "Bow, 'Frisk.' Bow!" at the same time firmly pushing the pony's head down, and before the first lesson ended "Frisk" had discovered that "Bow" meant bending his head as near the ground as possible and a prompt reward of carrots.

"It won't take long for 'Frisk' to learn," declared Ted; "by the time the twins get here we'll have taught him a lot of tricks. I hope that Janet won't try riding 'Patch' again."

"She won't! I'm sure she won't," Kathleen promised eagerly; "but I do want the twins to have a good time. Can't we have a make-believe circus, Ted, while they are here?"

Ted shook his head. "No, ma'am! Those girls would break their necks. Maybe we can have a play though," he added thoughtfully.

"What's a play?" questioned Kathleen.

"Oh, it's pretending to be other people: people in history, like Queen Elizabeth, and Oliver Cromwell; or else people out of books like Don Quixote and Sancho Panza," replied Ted, while his small sister gazed at him admiringly, thinking that Ted knew more than any other boy in the whole state, and that the idea of a play was the finest possible way to entertain Janet and Beth.

"Yes! Let's have a play!" she agreed, her blue eyes shining with pleasure. "Let's play I'm Queen

Elizabeth, and I'll dress up grand, in a crown and everything!" and remembering the golden dress (just what a queen would wear, thought Kathleen), the little girl skipped about as if practicing a new dance step.

But Ted shook his head soberly.

"No, we'll make up a play of our own," he announced.

"What about?" asked Kathleen.

"Oh, I'll think up something," Ted promised, — "a play so you can dress up as grandly as you want to," he added smiling at Kathleen's happy face.

"And Janet and Beth can be in it, too?" she asked, and Ted promptly agreed, and they started toward the house talking of possible characters for Ted's play.

It was that noon that Mr. Webb, just returned from a visit to Gettysburg, told them that the governor of Pennsylvania, the Honorable Andrew G. Curtin, had asked the cooperation of other states, whose sons had fallen in the Battle of Gettysburg, gallantly fighting for the Union, to set apart the field of battle as a sacred burial ground for all time.

"And it is likely that President Lincoln will take part in the consecration services," Mr. Webb concluded.

"Will we see him? And will General Lee come?" questioned Kathleen.

"'General Lee!'" repeated Ted, scornfully. "You ought to know better than that, Kathleen! The war isn't over, even if we did turn back the Confederates. Is it likely Pennsylvania would ask Lee to come back?"

"No, the war isn't over; but the Battle of Gettysburg has decided the struggle. It was the turning point of the Civil War. Even Jefferson Davis must now realize that no state has the power to defy the nation, and that our land is dedicated to human liberty. The conflict between North and South must soon end in triumph for the Union," said Mr. Webb, "and if President Lincoln finds it possible to come to Gettysburg it will add the final honor to that immortal field."

"Will we see President Lincoln?" asked Kathleen, nearly breathless with excitement at such a possibility, and for the moment forgetting even the golden gown and Ted's proposed play.

"Of course we will see him!" Mr. Webb replied smilingly. "And you may be sure if President Lincoln visits Gettysburg it will be a visit that will be remembered as long as the town exists."

Kathleen thought of this many times in the days that followed; and through all her plans for the twins' visit, and as she sat on the garden-seat happily stitching on the silver-blue cape for Adelaide Mary, even when teaching "Frisk" to copy all "Patch's" accomplishments, the little Yankee girl was looking eagerly forward, hoping that President Lincoln would really come to Gettysburg and that, as her father had promised, she would see him and hear him speak.

CHAPTER XVII

THE PLAY

EVERY day Kathleen questioned Ted about the "play."

"Can't I help make it up?" she would ask eagerly, and her brother would smile and say:

"Maybe. I remember you wrote verses for the May baskets, and as soon as I really decide what the play is to be about I'll tell you."

But although Kathleen made many suggestions Ted declared that he didn't want a play about queens.

"You just want to dress up," he said. "But I want a real play: like Columbus discovering America, or George Washington defeating Cornwallis."

"Those are not plays, they're history!" said Kathleen. "*I* want a truly make-believe play, with a queen in a golden dress, and a gypsy, and fairies that come and dance in the moonlight, and   and and everything!"

Ted laughed good-naturedly. "All right. Go ahead and make it up. I'll wager Janet and Beth will help you; they will want performing horses!"

Kathleen's face instantly brightened. "You'll help, whatever it is, won't you, Ted?" she asked earnestly, and Ted agreed, well pleased to escape the responsibility of creating a play that would please Kathleen and satisfy his own wish to represent some great figure in America's history; and the delighted Kathleen now made the big attic her chosen playroom; and with the big windows at each end opened wide the attic made as pleasant a place as any little girl could wish. The soft summer breezes, fragrant with the scent of flowers and ripening fruit, drifted in; and summer showers made music on the shingled roof as Kathleen wrote down her list of characters for her play and made up what each one was to say.

She had told her mother of this plan to entertain Janet and Beth, and Mrs. Webb declared that nothing could be better, and delighted her small daughter by reading her "A Midsummer Night's Dream," so that Kathleen was more sure than ever that a play must have fairies and a queen.

She had pulled a rickety old table close to the western window of the attic, and spread out her papers on it; and with Adelaide Mary established on a three-legged footstool near by, the little girl passed many happy hours imagining what a beautiful queen, in a golden dress, would do and say when she discovered that she was, after all, not a queen but a gypsy child whom the fairies had brought to the castle.

"Janet can be the gypsy, who is really the queen," decided Kathleen; "but Beth is too fat for a fairy!" And for days Kathleen puzzled about how the fairies of her imagination could become real, and when the first week in September brought Janet and Beth, accompanied by Miss Melvina, for the long expected visit Kathleen had completed her play, and was eager to tell the twins of the part they were to take.

But on their arrival Janet and Beth had so much to tell of the plans being made in Gettysburg for a visit by President Lincoln in the near future, that Kathleen had no opportunity to speak of her play.

"Mr. David Wills hopes that consecration services on Cemetery Hill can take place in October or early November, and that President Lincoln can surely be present," said Miss Melvina.

"He has chosen the right place. It was there that the Union artillery were massed, and where so many gallant soldiers met their death," said Mr. Webb, "and its consecration will be an occasion of national importance."

While their elders discussed the proposed memorial services so soon to be held for the gallant soldiers on the battle-field of Gettysburg, Kathleen with Janet and Beth slipped away and ran up to the attic. The golden dress and plumed hat had been returned to the black leather trunk, nor did Kathleen now speak of them, and the twins greeted Adelaide Mary, admiring her new cape and bonnet of silver-blue silk. They wanted to hear about "Patch" and "Frisk," and Kathleen promised that this time the twins should surely ride on her pony; but Hitty rang the supper bell before Kathleen found a chance to say: "Girls, I've written a play!" and promptly discovered that the twins knew exactly what a "play" meant, and that they, too, had become acquainted with the delights of "A Midsummer Night's Dream," and Janet eagerly inquired what name Kathleen had given her play; and Kathleen had just time to reply: "The Queen's Golden Gown," when Miss Mel called to them that supper was waiting.

"It's a secret—the name, I mean," Kathleen whispered as they entered the dining-room, and Janet and Beth both nodded soberly; and during the meal the three little girls exchanged frequent smiling glances of understanding, while their elders spoke of the recent victory of Union armies at Vicksburg, and of their hope that the great conflict between North and South would soon end in a lasting peace.

"Tell us all about 'The Queen's Golden Gown,'" urged Janet, as after supper the girls went to the pleasant room known as Kathleen's schoolroom. A little fire of birch logs blazed in the fireplace, and sitting on the big "hooked" rug before the hearth with Janet and Beth eagerly listening, Kathleen told them the story of her play.

"You see," she concluded soberly, "it's all the golden dress. Just the moment the queen takes it off she is only a gypsy, because the fairies carried the real queen, when she was a tiny baby, to the gypsy camp and carried a gypsy baby to grow up a queen."

"But you ought to have a truly grand gold-colored dress!" said Janet; and at this Kathleen was tempted to tell the twins all about the wonderful brocaded gown that glimmered and shone like sunlight itself; but, as she had resolved to keep this a secret until the queen appeared in it, she made no reply, and Janet asked: "Who is to be the queen?" and the surprised Kathleen answered quickly:

"Why, of course I'm going to be queen! I wrote the play," and she wondered a little that Janet and Beth did not at once say that of course Kathleen would have the finest part and wear the finest dress. But a little silence followed, and Kathleen at last said:

"And Janet is to be the gypsy."

"Then I'll be queen in the last act!" announced Janet, with such evident satisfaction that Kathleen began to feel uncomfortable, for she had not made her play end that way, and she now explained hurriedly:

"No. It's the golden dress, don't you see, that makes the queen. As long as she wears it she *is* queen. So she wears it all the time."

"What becomes of the *real* queen, who has to grow up a gypsy?" questioned Beth.

"Oh! She is so good to the fairies, putting honey on tiny glass plates for them each night, and making little warm shelters beside trees where they can stay when it is cold, that they make her a Fairy Queen, and she has a grand castle that she can move anywhere she wants to live by just repeating a verse," Kathleen explained, and Janet smiled approvingly and Beth asked what the verse was.

> "Gypsy and fairy may go where they please;
> To sea or to mountain they journey with ease.
> Their castles go with them all shining and fair—
> So now with my castle I'll sail through the air,"

repeated Kathleen, and Janet and Beth both looked at her admiringly, and Beth exclaimed:

"That's just like verses in books!" and then added: "What am I going to be in the play, Kathleen?"

Before Kathleen could answer there was a light tap on the door followed by Ted's voice calling: "Who wants to pop corn?" and corn-popper in one hand and a small basket filled with well ripened ears of corn, he came into the room declaring that the fine bed of hot coals was exactly right to pop corn, and in a few moments the tiny kernels were in the popper and snapping merrily as they blossomed into white delicious pop-corn.

Kathleen ran off to the kitchen for a big yellow bowl and butter, and the girls forgot about the proposed play as they happily crunched the delicious corn, and listened to Ted as he explained all the plans that Pennsylvanians were making for the consecration services of the battle-field memorial.

"And President Lincoln will be sure to come," the boy said, his face brightening at the thought that he might soon hope to see the great statesman who was to become the ideal of American manhood.

"Beth and I are both to have a new dress for that day," announced Janet. "We are going to spend our gold pieces to buy them. Miss Melvina says everyone ought to look their best in honor of President Lincoln."

"Nothing could be too good for him," said Ted gravely, "not even a dress of gold," and at this Kathleen made a quick resolve: If President Lincoln really did come to Gettysburg she would wear that beautiful golden brocade. She said nothing of this to anyone, but henceforth whenever anyone spoke of the President's visit Kathleen would again promise herself that the golden brocade should do honor to Lincoln and to the brave soldiers who, so short a time before, had given their lives at Gettysburg that the nation might live.

Mr. and Mrs. Webb and Miss Melvina joined the group before the fire and shared the pop-corn; and when they all said their good-nights and Kathleen and the twins started toward their rooms Beth found a chance to again whisper her question to Kathleen: "Who am I going to be in the play?" and the puzzled Kathleen could only whisper back:

"I'll tell you tomorrow."

CHAPTER XVIII

JANET'S DECISION

As Kathleen remembered her promise to tell Beth the part she was to take in "The Queen's Golden Gown" she felt a little troubled, and lay awake long after the twins were sound asleep wondering what she should say on the following morning when Beth would expect to be told.

"She's too big for a fairy, and Janet has to be the gypsy because her eyes and hair are dark, and of course I have to be queen. Oh, dear, I guess Beth will have to be the queen's maid. She can wear a cap and a big apron and make me a low bow and say: 'Your Golden Highness, the gypsy desires an audience,'" and delighted with so pleasant a way out of her difficulties Kathleen smiled happily and was soon fast asleep.

But Beth did not seem as delighted as Kathleen expected her to be when told of her part in the play. She did not say a word, nor did she even look at Kathleen as Kathleen eagerly explained: "It's the easiest part, Beth! Truly it is. You won't have to even study a bit; all you'll have to do is to bow low, like this," and with her arms extended Kathleen made a very low bow, "and then say: 'Your Golden Highness, the gypsy desires an audience.' Anybody could do that," Kathleen concluded, wondering why Beth's cheeks flushed so deeply, and why Janet looked at her so queerly, and why neither of them had a word to say.

"Katy-did! Katy-did!" Ted called. So she ran off to see what he wanted, saying: "I'll be right back, and then we'll begin fixing the throne under the oak tree, and I'll tell you about the fairies," and the twins found themselves alone.

"I want to go home," said Beth, tears gathering in her blue eyes as she recalled Kathleen's careless statement that Beth's part was of so little importance that anyone could take it. "I don't want to be in her old play. All Kathleen wants is to be the whole play. I want to go home."

"So do I!" declared Janet, even more angry than her sister. "Kathleen isn't going to let the real queen be queen at all. It isn't fair, and I don't want to be in it. But how can we go home, Beth? Miss Melvina wouldn't like it."

"We could just go," whimpered Beth.

But Janet shook her head soberly. "No. That's what Kathleen did just before the Battle of

Gettysburg, and frightened everybody. I'm going to tell Miss Melvina that we want to go home; that's the best way. You stay here until I come back," and without waiting for Beth to reply Janet darted out of the room to find Miss Melvina and explain as best she could, without telling of Kathleen's part in it, that she and Beth wanted to start at once for Gettysburg. She heard voices on the side porch and turned in that direction, thinking if Miss Melvina was there she would ask her to come in a moment; but just before reaching the open door she heard Ted's voice saying:

"Well, if I were Janet and Beth I wouldn't take part in your play. You want to be the whole show. A queen and a gypsy, and a maid and fairies! And you're the queen! That's a great play, that is," and Ted laughed scornfully, and Janet heard Miss Melvina's pleasant voice ask: "Do Janet and Beth like their parts?" and Kathleen responded:

"I didn't ask if they liked them. I just told them what they were to be."

"I see," said Miss Mel, and now Janet listened eagerly, quite forgetting that she was an eavesdropper, and when Miss Melvina said, "I rather think, Kathleen, that the twins are being more polite than you are," Janet gave a little gasp of satisfaction, and took a step nearer the door. "You see, they have accepted the parts you did not want to take, while you, their hostess——" At this Janet, who could now see not only Miss Melvina but Ted and Kathleen, heard Kathleen's half-smothered exclamation and saw that Kathleen was crying, and without waiting to hear another word she ran back to the weeping Beth.

"Stop crying, Beth, and wipe your eyes. Quick! Now listen! We don't want to go home. We mustn't! It wouldn't be polite. And Kathleen will be back here in a minute to ask you to be the queen; but——" Seeing Beth's face brighten Janet added firmly, "You can't be. That wouldn't be polite either! We're company. Whatever we do we must act like company; and when Kathleen says that you are to be queen in the first act and I am to be queen in the second act, we'll both say 'No.' Now remember, Beth! And we'll say we want Kathleen to be queen; because we do, really. It would be silly and mean to go home. You *know* it would, Beth," urged Janet, for Beth was still sniffing unhappily; but before Kathleen returned she had recovered her usual good nature and agreed with Janet that they could have as much fun as a gypsy and a waiting-maid as they could in the part of queen.

But Kathleen's face wore a most serious expression as she entered the room; for it had been a morning of many troubles. Her mother had asked her what she meant to wear as queen, and on hearing of Kathleen's discovery of the golden brocade had exclaimed that she had forgotten that the treasured gown was in the black trunk, and had said:

"Why, that gown is a family treasure, only to be worn on really great occasions! My dear girl, I'm so sorry, but I can't possibly let you have it for your play."

"Then there can't be any play," wailed Kathleen. "I made up the play to fit the dress. I'd be so careful, Mother," but Mrs. Webb shook her head.

"I'll make you a dress of yellow cambric. I have some in the house that shines like silk; that will have to do, dear," she said.

"Could I wear it if President Lincoln were coming here?" asked Kathleen, and Mrs. Webb smilingly replied that on so great an occasion as a visit from the President she might want to wear the golden dress herself, but added: "But I'll promise you shall wear it," and Kathleen reluctantly gave up her hope of wearing the beautiful gown in the play.

Directly after this had come Ted's and Aunt Mel's accusation of selfishness in keeping the best part in her play for herself, and Kathleen now returned to her visitors wishing that she had never even thought of a play.

"A circus with 'Frisk' and 'Patch' for trained hors-es, and Ted for a clown would be a lot more fun after all," she thought; but when she discovered that nei-ther Janet nor Beth would accept the part of queen, and when they both declared they thought their own parts just as good as hers, Kathleen's spirits bright-ened, and she told the twins that Ted had promised to have fairies appear at the right moment in the play, and that the throne under the oak tree was nearly finished.

"We'll have the play right after supper," she announced, thinking to herself that Janet and Beth Ross were the most pleasant girls in the world; nor did Kathleen ever learn of the twins' resentment of her thoughtlessness or even imagine how near they had been to starting for home.

The day passed busily and happily. Janet learned the verses Kathleen had written for the gypsy to say, and Beth practised the maid's bow so vigorously that she twice fell flat on her face to the amusement of herself and Janet and Kathleen; and Ted announced that he had, by great good fortune, persuaded a "tribe" of fairies to be on hand in good season; and after an early supper, the girls hurried away to make ready. Mrs. Webb had asked a number of neighbors to come and see what Kathleen and her friends would do with "The Queen's Golden Gown," and in the early dusk of the September evening a little group gathered on the porch facing the big oak tree.

There was a murmur of surprise when, from each side of the "throne," which was brightly lighted by a number of candles securely fastened by tin holders, there floated out a number of tiny figures that might well have been called "fairies," for Ted had cleverly made, of corn-floss, white cotton and leaves, a "tribe" of small winged figures. To each one he had attached a string, the other end being fastened to a limb of the oak, and by a connecting string he was able to make the "fairies" appear and disappear at his pleasure.

The cambric gown shimmered and glowed in the candlelight; the gypsy in a red gown, that Aunt Mel furnished, added a graceful dance to her part, and the waiting-maid bowed so low that she repeated her morning tumble, and at the close of the last act the queen stepped from the throne to take the gypsy by the hand and announced. "Here is the true queen———" And quickly lifting the golden robe from her own shoulders she placed it about Janet and disappeared in the shadow.

Everyone declared the play a success, and the "players," guests, and hosts returned to the dining-room for a cup of Hitty's fine chocolate and to enjoy the frosted cakes that Mrs. Webb had prepared for them.

The girls and Ted had a small table to themselves; and as Ted took his seat beside Kathleen he smiled on her approvingly. "You're a good soldier, after all, Katy-did," he said.

"That's what the Confederate scout said," Kathleen quickly responded: for, although weeks had passed since the battle of Gettysburg, all connected with it, Ted's escape through the Confederate soldier's kindness, as well as her own adventures, were never far from Kathleen's thoughts.

Beth chatted happily about the fairies, and Janet was well pleased to have been a queen in spite of herself, while Kathleen was completely happy and satisfied when she remembered her mother's promise that, if President Lincoln ever visited them, Kathleen should surely wear the dress of golden brocade.

She could hear the grown up people at the long table talking hopefully of the prospect of an early peace, and heard them speak of the prospect that President Lincoln would surely be present in

Gettysburg on the day set for the memorial services for the soldiers who had fallen.

"The day is now determined upon: it is to be the 19th of November," said one of the guests; and Kathleen repeated the date aloud:

"The 19th of November!"

"What's that?" questioned Ted.

"It's the day President Lincoln is coming to Gettysburg," Kathleen soberly replied.

CHAPTER XIX

PRESIDENT LINCOLN

THE days of the twins' visit passed quickly. To their delight they rode "Frisk" and "Patch"; they shared in the lessons in Kathleen's schoolroom, and helped her work on the "hooked" rug that she had begun, and that was to be exactly like the one she had given to the Confederate scout; and every day the little girls talked over the play and repeated the lines Kathleen had written; and every day Ted or his father rode to Gettysburg to learn of the progress being made in preparation for the day when seventeen Union states, whose sons had fallen on that battle-field, would send their chief executives to unite in the appropriate ceremonies of dedicating their burial place, and when President Abraham Lincoln, and his guard of honor, would be the guests of Gettysburg.

Ted was to drive the twins home, and Janet and Beth bade Kathleen good-bye declaring they had enjoyed every minute.

"'Specially 'The Queen of the Golden Dress,'" added the smiling Beth, who had that very morning confided in Janet that she was glad they had not gone home the day after their arrival at Webb farm, as the angry Beth had wanted to do.

"There is a truly golden dress, Beth," Kathleen had smilingly responded, "and some day you will see it!"

"When will I see it?" questioned the surprised Beth, who now was quite sure that Kathleen and Ted could accomplish whatever they wanted to do, and who was picturing to herself a gown of golden metal, instead of the shimmering brocade that Kathleen loved to think about and was so eager to wear.

"You'll see it when President Lincoln comes!" declared Kathleen, and Beth and Janet agreed that on that occasion it was to be expected that everyone would put on their finest apparel.

"We are to have new dresses, too," Janet reminded Beth, as they waved Kathleen adieu.

"I shall be in uniform again when the President comes," Ted proudly announced that night on his return from Gettysburg. "And Mr. Daniel Wills told me that the President is to stay at his house, and I am to be one of the guard!" and Ted tried very hard not to look too proud and pleased over this honor.

"Oh, Ted! Can I go with you?" pleaded Kathleen.

"Well, I should say *not*," Ted promptly responded. "Girls can't be guards; but," he quickly added, noticing Kathleen's disappointment, "you will be sure to see President Lincoln, and if he knows you were at Lee's headquarters during the battle of Gettysburg he may want a word with you," and Ted grinned cheerfully, for he often teased his small sister over the fact that she had helped a Confederate scout, and that she persisted in declaring her liking for the great Confederate general.

Kathleen made no reply; her thoughts were busy with imagining the solemn ceremony in which President Lincoln would take part. She remembered with a little thrill of pleasure that her mother had promised that on so great an occasion as a visit from President Lincoln it would be right and proper to wear the golden brocade; and as the days of sunny October passed and November came, and the time of Lincoln's visit to Gettysburg drew near, Kathleen's thoughts centered more and more on the possibility of doing some special honor to this great man, who had by his Emancipation Proclamation freed the negroes from slavery, and who was soon to rejoice in the surrender of Lee's army, and the unquestioned survival of national government.

"Mother, Ted is to be a guard on November 19th. What can I be?" she questioned, on the day when Lincoln was to reach Gettysburg.

"Why, my dear, a loyal little Yankee girl, such as you have always been," replied Mrs. Webb. "I know just how you feel, dear child," she added. "We all feel that we wish there was something splendid and beautiful that we could do for Lincoln; but it is our loyalty to his ideals that would please him more than anything; I am sure of that."

But to Kathleen this reply gave little help; she had gathered a large bunch of bitter-sweet, that grew near the ledge, and now asked if she could not give that to the President.

"It's something, anyway," she said, and her mother agreed that if there was a suitable opportunity she might give Lincoln the bitter-sweet; and with this promise, and the hope that the golden dress, and the plumed hat might be a sign of her wish to do him honor, Kathleen was obliged to content herself.

The special train bringing the President and his retinue reached Gettysburg on the afternoon of Wednesday, November 18th, 1863, and Ted, in a new uniform, was among the proud boys in blue who welcomed him. On the next morning all was stir and excitement in the town, and at an early hour Mr. and Mrs. Webb had driven in. They were to get Miss Melvina and then go to Cemetery Hill, where the exercises were to be, while Hitty was to take Kathleen in the pony-cart, starting at a later hour, and join them at an appointed place.

"The twins will probably come with us," Mrs. Webb told Kathleen as she bade her good-bye, and cautioned the little girl to start in good season, and Kathleen instantly fled to the attic to put on the golden gown and the plumed hat, and then decided it would be a good plan to wear the black cape also. "I can take it off if I do speak to President Lincoln," she thought, as she fastened the turquoise clasp that held the cape together.

"Fo' de lan's sake, Missy Kathy!" exclaimed the surprised and excited Hitty, as her young mistress came down the stairs, "where'd yo' fin' dat hat?"

But Hitty was too excited over the prospect of seeing the great Lincoln, the man who had given the colored race freedom from a debasing slavery, to pay much attention to what Kathleen was wearing. Hitty was dressed in her best, and eager to be on the way to Cemetery Hill, and Kathleen had just picked up her bunch of bitter-sweet and started toward the door when a sudden exclamation from Hitty made her look toward the highway at which Hitty was pointing.

"Look't! look't! My lan' an' hebbenly home! Dar dey come! De Pres'dent an' de army!" declared the excited Hitty, rushing from the room eager to reach the road over which the procession would march as soon as possible, and Kathleen was close behind her, unfastening the black cape as she ran so that the folds of the golden dress drifted about the little figure like sunlight, and the grave face of President Lincoln brightened a little as his glance rested on the queer little figure in a wonderful hat and a trailing gown that gleamed and shone as Kathleen, forgetting everything except that here was the great Lincoln, near enough for the little girl to see his smile as his glance rested upon her, ran toward him holding up the glowing bitter-sweet.

The President drew rein, and the procession, whose military part included Generals Schenck, Stahel, Stoneman and their staffs, came to a sudden halt; the measured drum-beats ceased, and the tall figure leaned from the saddle, to smile kindly down upon the little girl who had so fearlessly run toward him, and behind whom stood black Hitty gazing at him with worshipful eyes.

And now, at the great moment of Kathleen's life, as she gazed up into the grave patient face of Lincoln, she could think of nothing to say as he reached down and took the bitter-sweet from her hand.

"Thank you," he said gently, motioning to Hitty to draw her young mistress back from the highway, which the colored girl was quick to do, as the drum resumed its beat, and the procession moved on.

Neither Kathleen nor Hitty spoke as they turned back to the house, but as they reached the door Kathleen said: "We'll start in a minute, Hitty," and she quickly removed the brocaded dress, took off the hat, and when she seated herself in the pony-cart she was wearing the blue cashmere dress and embroidered cape that Aunt Mel had made for her.

But Hitty and Kathleen were late in reaching Cemetery Hill. Ted was on the watch for them and guided them to where Mr. and Mrs. Webb, Miss Melvina and Mrs. Ross and the twins were seated. Honorable Edward Everett of Massachusetts had finished his oration, a hymn had been sung, and President Lincoln was just beginning his dedicatory address; and sitting beside her soldier father the little Yankee girl again looked up at Lincoln and listened eagerly and earnestly to the eloquent address whose perfect simplicity even Kathleen could understand:

"Four score and seven years ago our fathers brought forth on this continent a new nation, conceived in Liberty, and dedicated to the proposition that all men are created equal.

"Now we are engaged in a great Civil War, testing whether that nation, or any nation so conceived and so dedicated, can long endure. We are met on a great battle-field of that war. We have come to dedicate a portion of that field as a final resting place for those who here gave their lives that that nation might live. It is altogether fitting and proper that we should do this.

"But, in a larger sense, we cannot dedicate—we cannot consecrate—we cannot hallow—this ground. The brave men, living and dead, who struggled here, have consecrated it, far above our poor power to add or detract. The world will little note, nor long remember what we say here, but it can never forget what they did here. It is for us, the living, rather to be dedicated here to the great task remaining before us—that from these honored dead we take increased devotion to that cause for which they gave the last full measure of devotion—that we here highly resolve that these dead shall not have died in vain—that this nation, under God, shall have a new birth of freedom   and that government of the people, by the people, for the people, shall not perish from the earth."

CHAPTER XX

THE END

As the Webbs drove toward home, Miss Melvina and the Ross family having returned to Gettysburg with friends, Kathleen sat beside her mother on the back seat of the carryall, while Hitty driving "Frisk" followed on behind.

"Mother, I gave President Lincoln the bitter-sweet; the procession came right by our house, and I ran out and gave it to him. He smiled at me, Mother; but he seemed sorry about something," said Kathleen, and added, "And I couldn't think of anything to say to him."

Mrs. Webb smiled at Kathleen's serious face.

"I am glad you could give him the bitter-sweet, dear," she said gently, "and it was like him to halt that procession to receive a gift from a child."

"And wasn't it lucky, Mother, that I had on the golden brocade?" Kathleen continued eagerly. "And I had on the plumed hat too. You know you said I might wear it, Mother, when President Lincoln came?" and Kathleen's glance rested a little ques-

186

tioningly on her mother, whose sudden exclamation: "The golden brocade!" made the little girl wonder if her mother had forgotten the promise.

"Oh, my dear girl! I meant if he ever came to our house——" but before Mrs. Webb could say more Kathleen had eagerly interrupted:

"But he came right past our gate! And you said yourself, Mother, that nothing could be too fine to do him honor; and you said the golden brocade was a treasure, and——"

But now Mrs. Webb interrupted, saying: "I believe I am as pleased that you wore the brocade as you are, Kathleen! For now it becomes a greater treasure than ever: your grandmother wore it when she was presented to the Queen of Italy, I wore it at a great ball in Philadelphia, but now its greatest value will be that it was worn by a little Yankee girl when the great Lincoln thanked her for a bunch of bitter-sweet. Yes, the golden gown shall be treasured more dearly than ever because you wore it to-day when Lincoln spoke to you."

Kathleen's face brightened happily, and she gave a little sigh of content as she rested her head against her mother's shoulder.

"I wish General Lee could have been here," she said, and at that her father turned a sharp glance toward her.

"Kathleen," he said gravely, "do you forget that you are a Yankee girl, and that General Robert Lee is the leader of the Confederate Army?"

"I guess he can't help that," responded Kathleen, "and he looked sorry, just as President Lincoln did," and Kathleen wondered a little at the glance that passed between her father and mother; but nothing more was said of Lee; and as the days passed and the Civil War ended in the triumph of the Union Armies, and when a letter came for Kathleen signed: "Claudia Summers," thanking Kathleen for the pine-tree rug that the little Yankee girl had given the Confederate scout, it was Mr. Webb himself who bade Kathleen be sure to answer the letter and to say that the Webb family would always gratefully remember the Confederate soldier's kindness to a little Yankee girl and to her soldier brother.

THE END